For Dorothy,

Dearest "Precious" heart —
mother to my heart.
God Bless your
journey!

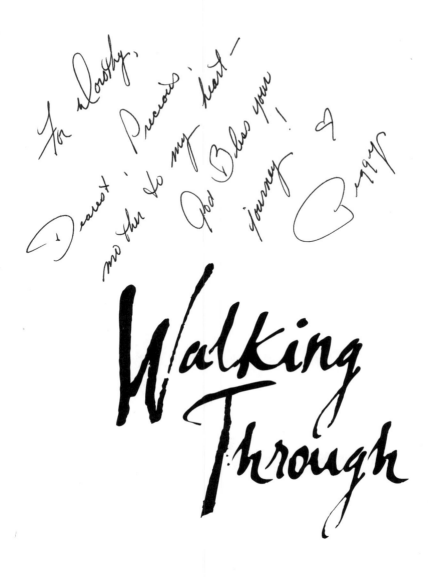

Walking
Through

PEG MUENZEL

Walking Through

HOPE FOR THE GRIEVING HEART

credo
house publishers

Published in the United States by Credo House Publishers,
a division of Credo Communications, LLC,
Grand Rapids, Michigan; www.credocommunications.net.

ISBN-10: 1-935391-39-9
ISBN-13: 978-1-935391-39-5

Unless otherwise noted, scripture is taken from the HOLY BIBLE,
NEW INTERNATIONAL VERSION®. NIV®. Copyright © 1973, 1978, 1984 by
International Bible Society. Used by permission of Zondervan. All rights reserved.

Cover and interior paintings: Peg Muenzel
Illustrations: Peg Muenzel

Cover and interior design: Michelle Krievins Newman
Interior layout: Virginia McFadden

Printed in the United States of America

TABLE OF CONTENTS

GRIEF MAP

The grief map is designed to help visualize grief as a place, a place
we can walk through.

DEDICATION

This book is dedicated to my precious family. Wayne, thank you for your constant patience as I struggled through the grief first for myself and again as I wrote. Kristine, Michelle and Andy, I trust that as you observed my pain over the loss of Jason, you realize that my love for you is no less. Often the pain I felt was as much for you because I know I wasn't the mother I wanted to be for many years. May God richly bless you for your understanding hearts. I love you more than words can say. Jason, the memory of your passionate enthusiasm for life filled with fun is an inspiration for me. I'm so glad God made you part of our family.

INTRODUCTION

Regardless of how we arrive in this strange new land of grief, there are parts of the terrain that everyone will experience. As I traveled through I "drew a map" with my journal in the hope of helping others who found themselves as lost as I felt. While I've used stories from my journey, this book is not intended to be about me or my family. The stories are intended to illustrate the territory. Because we all are so unique, my intent is not to give specific directions, but more an overview of the lay of the land with some personal insights gleaned on the journey.

When our hearts feel like the twin towers after 9/11, there is much work to be done to put a life back together. My prayer is this little book will keep you company on the path and give you encouragement and hope in your healing. No one should have to travel such a path all alone.

Some steps are bigger – some more confident ...

But the important thing is to keep walking.

KEY VERSE

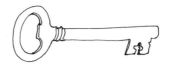

1 Thessalonians 4:13–18

Brothers, we do not want you to be ignorant about those who fall asleep, or to grieve like the rest of men, who have no hope. We believe that Jesus died and rose again and so we believe that God will bring with Jesus those who have fallen asleep in him. According to the Lord's own word, we tell you that we who are still alive, who are left till the coming of the Lord, will certainly not precede those who have fallen asleep. For the Lord himself will come down from heaven, with a loud command, with the voice of the archangel and with the trumpet call of God, and the dead in Christ will rise first. After that, we who are still alive and are left will be caught up together with them in the clouds to meet the Lord in the air. And so we will be with the Lord forever. Therefore encourage each other with these words.

ENTERING OUR VALLEY

Our entrance was sudden and shocking. On June 26, 1992, our 15-year-old son Jason was killed in a car accident. Michael, the driver of the car, was pronounced dead at the scene, and Brian, the lone survivor, is a paraplegic.

It was Friday and we were looking forward to Jason coming home from a week at Bible camp in northern Wisconsin. Plans for a vacation together as a family at Grandpa's cabin by a lake were gleaming brightly before us as summer kicked into full swing. Instead, late in the morning, I received a phone call at work. There were three people in the car, one of whom was dead. Jason had been air lifted to the Madison hospital. The doctor was not hopeful.

Wayne and I, along with Michelle and Andy, our two children at home, started the two hour drive to Madison, not knowing whether Jason would survive. Our eldest daughter Kristine and her husband Dan were counselors at the Bible Camp where the accident occurred. We will never know exactly what happened, but it seems Michael got permission for him and Jason to load their things in his car. Camp would be over right after lunch. So he got his keys to drive up to the cabin. The three boys then took what we presume was meant to be a quick spin out of the camp. Neighbors saw them leave. They were on their way back to camp when Michael lost control of the car. They were going fast, but it was a straight road. Was there a deer or another animal trying to cross? Did he swerve to avoid hitting something? One way or another, they hit a culvert, were airborne and crashed. A neighbor came to the scene and called for help.

Immediately after the phone call telling us Jason was in the hospital, we gathered our things together for what we assumed would be a lengthy stay in Madison, a two hour drive from home. Philippians 4:6-8 (NAS) says "Be anxious for nothing, but in everything by prayer and supplication with thanksgiving let your requests be made known to God. And the peace of God, which surpasses all comprehension, shall guard your hearts and your minds in Christ Jesus."

The truth of that verse was never more tangible. About 20 minutes into the trip the van was bathed in peace. We were praying, and all the kids at camp were praying. Word spread quickly and people all over Wisconsin were praying for Michael, Jason, Brian and our families. As this warm peace enfolded us, I heard the Lord gently whisper to my heart, "And the peace of God which passes all understanding will keep your hearts and minds in Christ Jesus."

We drove that way for more than an hour ... enveloped in this tangible peace. As we approached the outskirts of Madison, however, I became a little uneasy. What did this mean—all this peace? Was everything going to be all right or was I really in need of such tender care because there was tragedy beyond belief awaiting us? In an instant the answer came. As I gazed out my window, a moving painting unfolded. Monet himself couldn't have chosen a more tranquil scene. Observing the brilliant June blue sky, interrupted only by an occasional whisper of halo shaped clouds, I noticed farm machinery perched on a nearby hill. Then, oh so quietly the same still small voice whispered, "There's a time for planting and a time for harvest ... a time to live and a time to die." I didn't want to hear it. I didn't want to receive it. But I knew as I gazed from my seat in the van, that up above, just beyond the clouds, if I could just remove the veil, there were angels rejoicing as they do when a believer goes to heaven. I knew they were there, celebrating. I couldn't quite comprehend or completely grasp the truth I was being told. Jason wasn't here. He'd gone to heaven. The joy there was unmistakable. The courtyards were full of praise. I sat in silence, unable to accept the truth. God knew, even though it was impossible for me to grasp the truth completely, that I needed to know Jason was at home in heaven with Him right then. He was reassuring me.

Our arrival at the emergency room verified what I already knew. Unfortunately, we weren't told in a straightforward manner

"Your son did not survive." The doctor was busy with another patient, the nurse was too uncomfortable to tell us, or it wasn't her responsibility—the situation was confusing. Wayne and I were allowed to see Jason before we were told. He was in a curtained off portion of a large room; it was not at all private. He was hooked up to a ventilator and looked nothing like our darling boy.

Then we were taken back to a conference room where Michelle and Andy were waiting. The doctor came in and told us Jason was brain dead. The machine was only on to facilitate saving the organs for transplant recipients. The unbelievable truth: Jason was gone.

Jason was gone before we ever arrived at the emergency room. He was already being welcomed into the courtyards of praise, full of angels rejoicing over his homecoming.

He entered paradise. We entered the valley.

Ecclesiastes 3:1–4

1   There is a time for everything,
      and a season for every activity under heaven:
2   a time to be born and a time to die,
      a time to plant and a time to uproot,
3   a time to kill and a time to heal,
      a time to tear down and a time to build,
4   a time to weep and a time to laugh,
      a time to mourn and a time to dance …

Father, please be with each one who is walking through the valley of the shadow. Whether the cause is the sudden or prolonged death of a loved one, divorce, or another loss, you care. Please be their comfort and their guide. Bring them hope. Bring them friends to stand alongside. Most of all, Father, give them more of yourself, the great comforter. Thank you for being my constant companion. Amen.

Try to express your sorrow. Good punctuation and sentence structure are not the goal, just you pouring out your pain onto paper.

_____

_____

_____

_____

_____

_____

_____

_____

_____

_____

_____

_____

"Facing the truth is never easy
when the truth is that someone
you loved has died."

Entering the Jungle

It seemed as though I woke up each morning with a twisted mass of vines growing around me—truths I needed to deal with. Life would never be the same. Jason would never run down the steps to kiss me goodnight before bed or pick another fight with his brother. We would never laugh hysterically at his jokes or watch him play basketball. He would no longer hug me when I was sad or deliver papers to the neighbors. There would be no more birthday parties or late nights at the lake with him. There seemed to be no end to all the endings.

The changes in our home, mixed with the pain in my heart, felt like a dense cloud of humidity. It was a cloud of grief so thick it rivaled London fog in the winter.

Everything I thought and did had to pass through the knowledge that Jason was gone forever. His death surrounded every thought.

Every day the trail looked the same—vines overgrowing all my progress from the day before. I would take my machete and hack away at the truths before me. It was exhausting and extremely painful.

This beginning stage of grief, when everything is drenched in memories and the knowledge of your loss, lasts anywhere from three to six months. But, like fog on a beautiful day, it will lift. Slowly, there will be moments of relief; then hours followed by days. However, the fog lifting is not the end of grief. It is the beginning of the healing process.

When I first read that grief took three to five years, I thought, "I'll never be able to stand it that long." I thought this meant that the intense pain I suffered those first three months would continue for years. It doesn't.

As the fog lifts, grief becomes more like ocean waves. Sometimes it comes with crashing force when you least expect it. It knocks you down and takes your breath away. Sometimes it's more like a gentle wave lapping at your ankles, wetting your feet, making you aware of its presence, but not capsizing you. I hated how erratic those waves could be. Sometimes I felt just fine and then I'd see a little boy who reminded me of Jason at age three, or I'd hear one of his favorite songs on the radio, and I'd be a mess.

Grief is not a straight road from pain to healing. It's more like mending a sock. My mother taught me how. First, you cut away the jagged edges, making a neat hole. Then you take thread and make straight stitches covering the hole. The next step is weaving thread back and forth across the first straight stitches. This way the entire hole is filled in. Grief is like mending. Your heart and mind have to comprehend the loss. This takes going over and over the pain until you can fill in the gaps. One way to help in the process is to talk to people about it. There's something about hearing it from your own lips that is healing. If you don't want to trouble friends, try a support group or a counselor. I found understanding friends to be priceless in the process.

The fog scared me because I didn't understand that it would lift. Grieving annoyed me because I wanted to go through it all at once and be done with it. It just doesn't work that way. I had no control over my sadness, loneliness and pain. Some people say that time heals all wounds. I don't agree. Time itself can create bitterness, anger or self pity. Healing does take time, but it also takes hard work and good choices as you walk through the process of grief.

Journal—January
(Six months after accident)

I read Jonathon, You Left Too Soon *by Biebel. Two things helped. The author expounded on the initial reaction being in our mind. I thought of our initial reaction that Jason was with Jesus; we hurt, but he was fine. God would work this for good because that's who God is. Then Biebel explained that the next step is the emotional reactions, and they are not so kind—the pain, the deep, deep sorrow and sense of loss—that aching, yearning, awful depression. That is our emotions working themselves out, battling with our minds to come to terms with the reality we've been dealt. That is the most difficult. But the hope-*

ful part of that to me was his saying that the two will fuse, that you can return then, with your emotions in synch, to your initial response. What hope. It has helped so much. I do believe I'm starting to heal, and I'm so thankful. Biebel also said that you would know you were starting to heal when you could look at a picture of your departed loved one and instead of the pain of the loss feel thankfulness for having had him. It's starting. It's scary because I know I can't possibly be through with all the pain, but I feel so much better. I don't want to go back ... maybe I won't. Maybe it's like therapy, so painful at first, then hard work and struggles and some pain but not like at first. I pray that it may be so—for all of us.

Journal—Jason's birthday
(Six years later—this kind of pain would most often happen on special days like the anniversaries or holidays)

Oh, Lord, the pain was deep, deep, deep, deep today. It did feel good to sob in Michelle's embrace—I guess I hate to "go back" to the grief. But the truth is that there's no escaping it. It's here. I'm sad, so very sad. I miss you, Jason, so very, very much. It felt earlier like a gnawing, gripping pain; now I'm sad and TIRED. Oh, Lord, would you please hold me.

Journal—Today
(13 years later)

The pain does not overwhelm me often. I'm happy and content. Writing this book is about going back to my initial response; God will use this for good.

Proverbs 4:18
The path of the righteous is like the first gleam of dawn, shining ever brighter till the full light of day.

Father, wherever they are in their process today, please hold them and comfort them. Amen.

How are you feeling today? Are you still in the grief fog? Are there gentle waves of sorrow today, or are you feeling overwhelmed by huge, crashing waves?

_____

_____

_____

_____

_____

_____

_____

_____

Mending a heart
means working through
the pain ...

A Prayer

Tender Jesus, meek and mild,
Come and bless this little child.

Surround her now with steadfast love
As your angels watch above.

Give her peace and quiet rest.
Hold her close into your breast,

Bringing peace all through the night
Until we wake to morning light.

(Author unknown)

THE BATTLE

It didn't matter what I wore. As I stared blankly into my closet, I wondered if anything would ever matter. I knew what lay ahead today, and I was in no hurry to participate. Prepare for Jason's funeral. How could this be? How could I face everything that would need to be done? I didn't want to go to the funeral home. I didn't want to choose a casket for my son. I didn't want to choose memorial folders. I didn't want to choose flowers. I didn't want to get dressed and go on. NO. NO. NO. How could this be? Bury our son? I barely slept the night before. Every time I nodded off, trying to escape the pain, I would be startled awake by a nightmare of Jason in the emergency room.

Overwhelmed with pain, choosing something to wear seemed senseless.

The thought slipped into my mind: "I could just turn around, crawl back into our bed, stay there and die." Everyone would understand. "It's just too much for her," they'd say, "She loved him so." Immediately, the Holy Spirit gently whispered encouragement, "Yes, you can give up or you can lean into the ever-loving arms of your heavenly Father, trust Him to hold you and comfort you and help you every step of the way." There was only one wise choice. What would be the purpose of giving up? What glory would that bring God? What legacy to my sweet boy? I knew that if I crawled back into bed instead of moving on, I would be setting a precedent. Would I listen to my screaming flesh or choose God's gentle, loving encouragement?

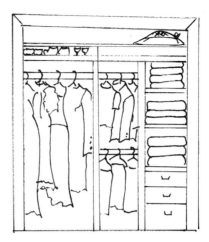

This was the beginning of my choice to go on. For me the temptation was always there to give up and go back to bed. There were times a good nap was necessary, but on this day and so many others it wasn't the sleep I craved but the avoidance of life.

My journal from that summer says it best:

But the decision to go on, to face life, that is the difficult part in all of this. If I could just grieve and not have to face living, if I could just not deal with people and decisions and the sunshine and the future—but daily I have to choose life or death, to give up and die inside or, with God's help, to go on.

There were days when the grief overwhelmed me, and I didn't always choose wisely. But God didn't give up on me. He was always there, comforting and guiding. His word says, "I can do all things through Christ who strengthens me." It's true. One day, one hour, one minute at a time God would help me. The choice was mine, the strength completely his. I did go on that first morning. I continue going on each day. Now the joy has over-come the mourning.

Romans 5:5
And hope does not disappoint us, because God has poured out his love into our hearts by the Holy Spirit, whom he has given to us.

Philippians 4:13
For I can do everything through Christ who gives me strength. (NLT)

Dear Lord, sometimes it hurts so badly I think I can't stand it. Help me to choose wisely. Give me the strength I need to go on. Thank you that your Holy Spirit speaks hope to my heart. Help me to hear you and trust you to take me through each day. I need you, Lord. Help me this day to choose life. Amen.

Are you choosing life or death?

_____

_____

_____

_____

_____

_____

_____

_____

_____

_____

COMFORT VALLEY

I wasn't afraid of the church service, but the funeral home was a different thing altogether. I just could not imagine seeing our precious son in a coffin. Horrible. Outrageous. So when our little family arrived for an early viewing, I was not prepared for what met me. Peace. Comfort. Relief.

Jason's body was there. He was not. It was not him lying in that box. I knew he was in heaven with Jesus. When our friends began to arrive, there was another shock. Wayne and I were the ones doing the comforting. "What is this?" I questioned God. Immediately the reply came to the depths of my being; "Comfort them with the same comfort I have comforted you."

So for six hours we stood and with peace shared the confidence that not only is Jesus alive, but Jason is too. His body, broken here, is not the final answer. The real Jason, the one we know and love, is in heaven. We will touch him and hold him again. Heaven is real. This separation is temporary. Before a child is born they cannot imagine a different world from the womb they are in, warm and soft and safe. In the same way, we cannot imagine being birthed through death into the new world Christ has for those of us who call on his name. Death is not the end. For believers, it is the beginning of the rest of our lives in heaven with Christ.

One visitor, a counselor, from the camp where Jason had his accident, gave me a priceless gift, a letter from Jason. I waited until I was home, in bed, alone, to read it. It was written in pencil, intended only for Jason's eyes, an assignment from his camp counselor who planned to mail it to Jason in about six months. Here is part of that precious letter:

Camp verse:
Galations 2:20b–21a
I live by faith in the Son of God, who loved me and gave himself for me. I do not set aside the grace of God.

I just want to tell you that I had a great time at Alive [the camp name]. I met a lot of new friends that are great. I rededicated my life to Jesus. I'm going to try to keep on track. Jason remember to read the Bible and stay close to God. Talk to him (pray) get together with Dan [his brother-in-law and youth pastor] and just talk about things. Somehow I must try to witness to my friends.

The last line is key: "Somehow I must try to witness to my friends." I'm thankful Wayne and I had the opportunity to hug his friends and tell them Jesus is alive and heaven is real. It's what Jason wanted. I'm thankful this means our separation is temporary. Even if it's 50 years, in light of eternity it's just a blip in time. For eternity we will be together.

2 Corinthians 1:3–4
Praise be to the God and Father of our Lord Jesus Christ, the Father of compassion and the God of all comfort, who comforts us in all our troubles, so that we can comfort those in any trouble with the comfort we ourselves have received from God.

Dear Lord, please comfort all who read this at their deepest point of need. Amen.

What do you need God to do for you today?

_____

_____

_____

_____

_____

_____

P. S.
Is your deepest need to know that your loved one is waiting for you with Jesus?

We were blessed to know beyond a shadow of a doubt that Jason is in heaven waiting for us. What if I weren't sure? I pray this won't sound simplistic or flip. I've thought about it often, because the question is real, and one I've dealt with, but not about Jason. For what it's worth, here is my thought process. I would choose to believe he/she had become a Christian before they died, even if it was at the last second. The separation is hard enough to deal with here, but the thought that my loved one might be spending eternity in hell would be too much for me to bear here. So I've chosen to think they may have made a choice I know nothing about and are waiting on the other side for me. The Bible gives us an example we can cling to. The thief on the cross next to Jesus believed in Him in the last moments of his life, and Jesus said, "Today you will be with me in paradise." That thought is so comforting. If I am wrong, and they chose to reject Him, I'll find out soon enough. At that point God himself will be there to wipe every tear from my eye and grant me grace to deal with separation if necessary. Why torture myself with something there is no answer to now? For me, it is better to believe and hope for the best. Only God knows another person's heart. I leave it in His hands.

Is your deepest need to know that you have eternal life with Christ?

To be honest, the foundation of this book is that you already know Jesus as your Lord and Savior. I don't want to do a disservice to those of you who may not understand what I mean by that. I believe that God the Father, Creator of the universe, has a Son whose name is Jesus. Jesus' life is well documented. He claimed to be the Messiah, the Savior of the world. I believe Him. He was crucified on the cross for our sins. He was buried and on the third day he rose from the dead. He spoke to his disciples and before their very eyes, returned to heaven. He says in his Word, the Bible, that if we confess our sins and believe on Him we will be saved. (Saved from an eternity separated from Him, saved to a new life with Him.) He also said that it would be better for us that He left, because then the Father would send the Holy Spirit, who would give us power, comfort, and direction and teach us. I am living proof that this is true. Without Jesus, without the love of the Father and the Holy Spirit, who is my comfort and guide, there would be no book. I would have given way to despair long ago. But instead I have the love and peace and joy Jesus promises His disciples.

I remember the day I prayed something like this, "Dear Lord, I believe you died for my sins. Thank you. Thank you for loving me. Please forgive me for how I've lived my life. Please come into my life and save me. I want to live my life for you." These were simple words that God honored. Jesus came as He promised. My life is forever changed and I am so grateful. I look forward to eternity with Him as He promises in His Word.

John 3:16
For God so loved the world that he gave his one and only Son, that whoever believes in him shall not perish but have eternal life.

Tell God what's on your heart.

_____

_____

_____

_____

_____

_____

_____

HEAVEN IS REAL

The Sunday morning after Jason's accident, Wayne took a walk down our quiet city street. He was on the sidewalk under the neighbors' huge spreading maple tree when he "saw and heard" Jason. He was jumping up and down and yelling, "It's true, Dad! It's true! Heaven is real!"

The Bible confirms Wayne's experience. Jesus said that He was going to prepare a place for us and that He would come again to receive us unto Himself. What a precious promise.

John 14:2–3

In my Father's house are many rooms; if it were not so, I would have told you. I am going there to prepare a place for you. And if I go and prepare a place for you, I will come back and take you to be with me that you also may be where I am.

Father, thank You for the promise of heaven forever with You. Thank You that I know Jason is waiting there to celebrate with us. Lord, for those who are uncertain of their own destiny, I pray You will bring them to a personal relationship with You and give them reassurance of their salvation. And for those who are worried about their loved one's eternity, please comfort them with Your precious compassion and grace and the truth that You alone know each one's heart. Amen.

How real is heaven to you?

_____

_____

_____

_____

_____

_____

A HEALING PRAYER

(Two days after the accident)

Sunday morning we were eager to get to church, but we waited until the last minute so we could slip into the back. We didn't want to make a big spectacle, but we needed desperately to be with our church family. As we slid into our seats, we realized there was a new couple sitting next to us. When the pastor spoke of the accident that claimed the lives of Michael and Jason and critically injured Brian, a boy from Madison, the woman by my side mouthed to me "That's our boy." We embraced and shed some tears. Then Pastor Clarence prayed ...

"Heavenly Father, we come into your presence today with troubled hearts. You know all about the accident that claimed the lives of Mike and Jason and critically injured Brian. We know you don't cause accidents or send tragedies that injure or kill people. But they still come unbidden into our lives. We know it is Satan who comes to steal and kill and destroy. Some day Jesus will return to earth and cast Satan and his followers into the lake of fire. But until then, he does cause misery wherever he can.

"Father, when tragedies like this happen, we are troubled and confused. We don't know what to say to the families who have suffered such a devastating loss. O Lord, we know that you are the only source of comfort and hope. You alone can mend broken hearts and broken dreams. So we simply lift up before you right now each of these suffering families. Gather them up in your strong and gentle arms, and hold them as they shed their tears. One great day in heaven you will wipe away every tear, and there will be no more sorrow or pain or suffering or death, for the former things will have passed away. But even now you can comfort these families because you can enter into their sorrow. You also saw your only Son die on a cruel cross for our sakes. And Lord Jesus, we remember your gracious invitation, 'Come to me all you who are weary and burdened, and I will give you rest. My peace I give you. I do not give you as the world gives. Do not let your heart be troubled, and do not be afraid.'

"Lord, help us to enter into the sorrow of these three families in the days and weeks and months ahead. You told us to rejoice with those who rejoice and weep with those who weep. You also told us to bear one another's burdens and so fulfill the law of Christ. Lord, by your Holy Spirit, speak through our halting words, and work through our loving deeds, to show your love to these three grieving families. For we pray it in Jesus' name, who shares all their pain and sorrow. Amen."

Psalm 54:2
Hear my prayer, O God; listen to the words of my mouth.

Dear Lord, for each hurting heart reading these words, will You comfort them as You did us, through others and especially through Your constant attention to our pain.

Are there people praying for you?

_____

_____

_____

_____

_____

"When you are hurting,
God gives you God."

THE AMPUTATION

If my leg were amputated, I would not expect to run a marathon any time soon. Much healing would be necessary. The nerve endings would be oh so sensitive. Fitting a prosthesis and getting used to it would be a huge and important task. I would need physical therapy and lots of love and support. This could take a long time. A marathon would have to wait.

The hole in my heart, though invisible, would take at least as much time, effort and loving care in order to heal properly. I was impatient with myself and with others who did not understand the huge effort it took to take just one more step. The healing would take time, effort and wise choices.

Attending a 10-week grief group was helpful. A counselor led the sessions. We watched videos, shared our stories, and did homework assignments. It was hard work, but valuable. It was a safe place to be in pain. I learned a lot about the grieving process, and it was good to be able to encourage others. It's like physical therapy for the soul.

I didn't go to an individual counselor, although I think I would have benefited from one. There were choices I made and thoughts that plagued me that I think a trained counselor could have walked me through more quickly. My reasoning for not going went something like this: "Unless they've lost a child, they won't have a clue." Now the counselor we had for our group hadn't lost a child, but she was helpful. I wasn't thinking logically. Individual counseling might have speeded up the recovery. It would have been like having a good physical therapist for a leg amputation. They know the basics; they don't need to have suffered the exact injury in order to be wise and compassionate.

So I struggled through the pain in my journals. The writing was a good outlet. I could pour out my grief onto those pages and not afflict those who loved me with my frustrations. Jesus walked beside me. He was my encourager, protector and guide. Jesus is a great heart mender. I learned to walk again, mostly without pain. Sometimes now I run marathons.

Psalm 18:6

In my distress I called to the LORD; I cried to my God for help. From his temple he heard my voice; my cry came before him, into his ears.

Lord, it's such a struggle to go on in this pain. Please help. Thank You that You hear my hearts' cry. Amen.

What are you struggling with today? Do you need to tell a friend, write in a journal, call a counselor, or cry in Jesus arms?

_____

_____

_____

_____

_____

_____

_____

_____

_____

"Forward motion, taking a step into the light and wind is imperative to stay connected to the almighty force of the creator of the universe."

I Can Hear Your Heart Beat

I can hear your heart beat

When I put my head on your chest.

I can hear your heart beat

When I crawl into your arms and rest.

When I crawl into your arms and listen

I can hear your heart beat.

Intimacy
Original Oil 36" x 30"

BLAME CITY

(Remembering the day of the accident)

Wayne hung up the phone. The doctor on the other end held out little hope that Jason would survive. "There will be no blame," Wayne said adamantly. It was an uncharacteristically strong word from my ever humorous, gentle husband. My mind reeled. His words stung. "No blame?" I could think of plenty of places to put blame. Though my heart screamed at me to comply with my pain, I knew I needed to listen to Wayne. Blaming would not be an option.

We're both convinced these words were right from God. There would be no lawsuits, no arguments, no accusations, no "I told you ..." This was a costly choice. It was painfully difficult to ignore the thoughts and temptation to "go down that road." That doesn't mean the thoughts did not come but that we chose to "take the high road." There certainly were times when we wished we could blame anybody, ourselves included. If blaming someone would have brought Jason back, I'd have been the first one in line. But all blaming would have done is cause more pain.

This decision, we are certain, kept our lives open to the free flow of God's healing grace. If we had chosen to blame and had harbored unforgiveness in our hearts, we would have missed out on the peace and comfort that our heavenly father so graciously poured out upon us. We're positive that this path made it possible for us to walk through our tremendous loss with any sort of sanity intact. God can't work through us if we harbor unforgiveness. It is totally against who He is. Jesus, on the cross, said "Father forgive them for they know not what they do" (Luke 23:24). Lack of forgiveness separates us from God and others.

There would have been only two good solutions to the problem of this loss. One would have been for Jason to come back; the other was for me to live in peace, love, and joy. Jason I will see in heaven, but my peace, my joy, my life cannot be lived to the fullest as long as I harbor unforgiveness.

I'm not saying that justice shouldn't be done. It should. But in order to experience peace with God and ourselves, forgiveness is imperative. Forgiveness is not necessarily reconciliation. It is not being a doormat. It is releasing yourself from carrying around the added burden of bitterness.

Blame leads to bitterness and more pain. It gives the enemy an opportunity to mess with our lives. Forgiveness opens the door to fellowship with God, the only One who can bring total peace and healing.

Ephesians 4:26–27

In your anger do not sin. Do not let the sun go down while you are still angry, and do not give the devil a foothold.

Father, when the pain is so deep it's easy to blame. Father, please help those who are struggling to deal with forgiving their loved one or others. Help them to release themselves from the pain of bitterness that grows when there is no forgiveness.

Is there anyone you need to forgive? Try to journal your pain.

_____

_____

_____

_____

_____

_____

"It's never too early to do
something that needs to be
done eventually!"

PRAYER MOUNTAIN

(One day after the accident, visiting Nancy, the mother of the driver.)

Saturday evening our goal was to reassure Nancy; we assumed her heart would be anxious and distraught. Wayne and I wanted her to know that we would never sue. There was enough pain without that. Nancy's son, Michael, the driver of the car, had died instantly. Since we had never met her, it seemed strange to go to her home for the first time as a result of such tragedy. Our boys had met at the church youth group and had become friends. Now, we would meet to share with her the words God had given Wayne on Friday: "There will be no blame."

We didn't have to go alone. Our daughter Kristine and her husband Dan would introduce us. Dan was the youth director. Nancy greeted us on the porch. We hugged and we cried. Then we went inside as Wayne gently reassured her there would be no lawsuit.

After some time together, Dan and Nancy went into the next room to speak privately. This left Wayne, Kristine and me alone for the first time since this nightmare had begun. We had been together most of the day, and Friday evening too, but always surrounded by groups of people. My heart was aching for Kristine; she was devastated. She felt so responsible. Of course she wasn't, but as the oldest sibling she had always helped take care of the little ones. She was a natural mommy. Now she was going to be a mother. Our first grandchild was due in about four and a half months. As we hugged and cried, she told us about Jason's week. He had had a wonderful time at camp. She and Dan were convinced it was the best week of his life. He had made lots of new friends, enjoyed all the activities, learned much in chapel and small group, and had recommitted his life to Christ. Kristine was his meal table counselor so she had been with him every day.

As she shared, she sobbed. We embraced as our tears flowed. When her anguish became extremely intense, I feared for her unborn baby. She was so tired. It was after ten o'clock and she had had almost no rest the night before. Every time she would fall asleep, she would have the same dream: Jason was having so much fun at camp, laughing and being silly; then she would hear brakes squeal and see the skid marks on the road and wake up horrified. I could certainly relate. I hadn't slept either. Every time I would doze off in an effort to escape the pain, I would startle to see Jason as he had looked in the emergency room. I would awaken then to the reality of the nightmare. We were all exhausted.

At that point, I looked to Wayne. Would he please pray for us? We had to get some rest; we needed some sleep this night. Kristine hugged my neck as I knelt by her chair; Wayne, on his knees beside me, arms around us both, prayed. His gentle words embraced us like the love of our heavenly Father. My heart was begging for rest and for a new picture.

That night, Kristine and I both slept. I awoke the next morning after about four or five hours of uninterrupted rest, thanking God for the respite from the grief and for the much-needed sleep. As I lay there talking to the Lord, he gave me a new picture. I was standing by the kitchen window; then Jason came in and took my hand. He had me turn around and sit at my usual kitchen chair. Then he got down on his knees, looked up at me, and said, "I'm sorry, Mom." With much difficulty, I replied, "Oh, Jason, it's all right. I forgive you." Then he put his head in my lap and let me play with his hair, as I gazed at his face.

Philippians 4:13
I can do all things through Him who strengthens me. (NAS)

Oh Lord, thank You for the new picture. You know how often I have looked back to that morning, thankful for the results of all the forgiveness You put into our hearts. Whatever the struggle Your dear one is facing, help them reach out to You. Amen.

What is your most urgent need? Who will you ask to pray for you?

_____

_____

_____

_____

_____

_____

_____

_____

_____

_____

The thought "My loved one died" is never very far from the surface. Maybe that's why small talk is so hard. There isn't much "surface" there; you very quickly bump into raw nerves.

LIE PIT

My insides felt like a caged tiger, pacing, pacing, looking for a way out of the pain. My heart was screaming into the universe, "Where is my baby? Where is my baby?!" All day long there was such emptiness in my heart and a deep longing for Jason; I thought I might go insane. There was an all-consuming blackness, chewing me up from the outside in. Emptiness was everywhere. He was lost, gone forever. I screamed, but no one answered. I felt completely alone in my grief, utterly and thoroughly alone. Screaming, screaming inside, my head pounded out the rhythm: This is hopeless, and there's nothing to be done. There was too much pain.

My pastor's words from weeks earlier reached out to help me. "If you ever need to talk," Pastor R. A. Pegram had offered, "Francis and I take a walk every night. Just call and come walk with us." They were always serving generous portions of love to everyone at Faith Church. This day, I needed them.

Wayne and I met R. A. and Francis in the early evening. As we strolled the rural road overlooking the entire valley, surrounded by the stars and the love of these two dear ones, I told Francis of my pain and hopelessness. She listened closely, then looked at me with her sweet, gentle face and said firmly, "That is right from the pit of hell. I'm going to pray this is the worst day you ever have."

God answered her prayer. That *was* the worst day of grief I ever experienced. I am convinced that it was necessary for me to live through that nightmarish day. I needed to understand how it would be to face this kind of loss without the Lord and the love and prayers of his people. I am so thankful they took the time to comfort us and speak truth to our hearts.

The truth is—the enemy goes around like a roaring lion, seeking whom he can devour. He has been a liar from the beginning.

The truth is—I do know where Jason is. He isn't lost. He's in heaven.

The truth is—I am not alone. The Lord is with me. There is love and comfort for me. I don't have to bear the pain alone.

The truth is—this separation is temporary.

The truth is—prayer does change things.

1 Peter 5:8–11

Be self-controlled and alert. Your enemy the devil prowls around like a roaring lion looking for someone to devour. Resist him, standing firm in the faith, because you know that your brothers throughout the world are undergoing the same kind of sufferings. And the God of all grace, who called you to his eternal glory in Christ, after you have suffered a little while, will himself restore you and make you strong, firm and steadfast. To him be the power for ever and ever. Amen.

Dear Lord,

I pray that You will comfort each dear one who is crying out to You right now. Speak the truth to their hearts: They are not alone. Protect them from the evil one and his lies. Give them the help they need to walk through the pain. Thank you for your loving care. Amen.

Have you listened to lies? What's the truth?

_____

_____

_____

_____

_____

_____

_____

_____

PRAYER ~ TALKING TO GOD

I use the definition for two reasons; first because in Jason's letter from camp he defined prayer as talking to God and second because I think we need to be reminded that prayer isn't some religious exercise but a wonderful privilege of communicating with the God of the universe.

The Psalms are full of David crying out to God. I used those Psalms to help me cry out as well. When David referred to his enemies I pictured those same enemies as death and grief. It comforted me to pour my pain into God's heart.

Listening to God's voice through his Word and in my spirit as I sought His presence and comfort brought me peace and joy in the darkness of the valley: peace because He held me, joy because He loved me.

Sometimes, when the burden was too heavy, a dear one would pray with me, for me, over me. What a gift! Jesus said that wherever two or more are gathered, there is He in their midst. What a promise! What hope!

Many prayed for me. I'm sure their prayers are still being answered as this book comes to completion.

Matthew 11:28
Come to me all who are weary and burdened and I will give you rest.

May God restore the years the locust have eaten, may you be filled to overflowing with joy unspeakable. May your hearts be light and your lives be full. May the God of all comfort be your shield and your high tower. Amen.

Try sitting on His lap and telling Him everything; then be still and listen.

_____

_____

_____

_____

_____

_____

_____

_____

_____

_____

_____

TRAIL NOTES ~ JOURNAL ENTRIES

September

It's been three months—Thank you, Lord, for a wonderful day. Took Andy to a Brewers game—it rained the whole way down—looked like we'd be rained out. But it cleared shortly after the game started. We won. It was great. Thank You especially for all the wonderful memories on the way home. Things I hadn't thought of for so long.

October
(Four months)

Yesterday was Jason's 16th birthday. I'm so incredibly sad. I went to the cemetery alone at dusk. I sobbed. My head aches so.

December
(Six months)

This is the hardest thing I've ever been through. It's not just the intense sense of loss—of my longing, yearning for Jason. I want to hold him—my insides long to clutch him close to me. My feelings are so sensitive. When I have a need, a need to express myself, I can't. Nobody gets it. Lord! I appreciate You so much more. You're the only One who knows my heart and truly understands my pain and loss. And You're the only one who won't let me down!

Read a good book last night ...
Poem from *Up the Golden Stair* by Elizabeth Yates.

Time is a test of trouble,
But not a remedy.
True, True! It isn't time that makes it better. It's me getting stronger—choosing to be. Time left to itself would accomplish nothing. Give credit where it's due. To God and true grit! I like this one, too:

And always mine, your love to hold,
To have no need to weep.

I'm not there yet—the having no need to weep. (After seven years I could say I have no need to weep ... I'm thankful.)

February
(Eight months)

Daily I need to reaffirm the reality of heaven and Jason's presence there and our ultimate endless eternity with no more sorrow. Part of the beginning being easier was that there wasn't

so much past to drag along. I mean day to day to day—it's tire-
some, the fluctuations of emotions are exhausting, and the going
back to the pain when you've had a respite is also exhausting.
Tiresome, wearisome, discouraging, heartbreaking. So then I run
to God; like I need to right now. And He'll hold me!

April
(Ten months)

Response to a friend's call ... I explained a little to her how the
tears, when I am asked, are not a pain that's being inflicted but
rather a release. The pain is there—it's not something someone
else does to me! When friends give me an opportunity to share,
they're assisting in the healing. It's like a wound that's infected
and red and swollen—the tears that flow are a healing balm—
but it's very hard sometimes to release them on your own or
maybe not as helpful—like having to bandage your own wound.
The person who asks and listens is the instrument used to release
the healing balm—very precious and appreciated. If I were
afraid of the pain and didn't move into it, I don't know how it
would go. I'm proceeding on the premise that tears are healing.
That when someone speaks of or asks about my sorrow, it is not
new pain but rather an indicator of what's going on under the
surface. How well the healing has progressed.

Dear Lord, thank you for showing me this morning how foolish
and ridiculous it is for me to blame myself for that accident.
THANK YOU! So, broken-hearted, I go on.

... I know I'm getting better because other things can irritate
me.

... I've worked my way through a lot of jungle. But when I hit
a clearing ... I don't know which way to go. I feel lost.

... Man, it is so hard to believe. What an irritating feeling.
But I need to relax in it. So it's hard to believe—of course it is.
And the more I fight the feeling, the worse it is.

... The sorrow reassures me of my love for him.

... The pain makes me run to God, to call to Him for help and answers, which he graciously supplies.

Lord, can't some things at least be easy? I know it's unrealistic. But it just seems like You should be able to skip some of the normal life junk—like I should have this card that I hand in, "a GET OUT OF JAM FREE card—no further trials necessary."

Eleven months

I asked the Lord what He wanted to show me by this "turmoil" that would come over me when I had to face the simple things of life again—even small changes in plans. "His answer: That's part of living again. What happens in spring? The sun shines, then it rains, then it's warm, then it's cold. Don't be startled by the changes. That's starting to live again." The weeping—the joy—the sun and rain.
Yesterday I asked the Lord to give Jason a hug for me. Then I thought—oh it would be nice if every time I thought of him the Lord would give him a hug. Then the Lord said that He and Jason think of me more. So every time I send a hug thought to him, I should receive one here.

About one year

... It's been over a year—incredible. It feels as though it happened yesterday—the sadness—like it's been forever—the loneliness for him—his smile, his touch, his laugh, that cute body, his beautiful eyes and hair. Oh, Lord, how I miss that boy.

The pain over the last month was like going through it all over again—only this time alone. I know people were praying and some tried to be there for us, but basically you have to do this alone, and it's hard and it hurts. It feels as though the Lord carried me that whole first year, and now I have to walk again, or like after major surgery. It's hard work, exhausting to get to the point where you're well enough to do everything. And then when you can, it's so hard. Everything takes effort.

I know from the outside I may look OK, but I'm tired, my brain is so slow to react, and relationships are strained with all but a few.

Today is our 26th anniversary. I had forgotten entirely until a card came in the mail yesterday. Lord, I need Your presence to be felt today. I read Psalm 119, cried to the Lord, ran to His shelter.

God showed me this: The focus has been on the pain, and that's OK. There's a bigger picture, though, and because the pain is so in focus, the rest is blurred and out of focus and that makes it hard to see.

This pain really is physical—my heart aches. There is a bigger picture.

If I try to broaden what's in the frame—purposely back up—it puts more into view, but it also helps to put things in focus. I'm trying to broaden my outlook. If I focus on the pain only, that's all I'll see. Help, Lord. Help me make the adjustment. I don't know how.

"You have to back off from some of the painful things to focus on the beautiful."

After a visit with a dear missionary friend home on furlough ...

She listened and prodded and encouraged me to share. When she prayed for me I realized afresh that this is the nicest thing people can do. Listen intently and pray precisely. She prayed for me to have hope and a reason to live again and for all our family and all the specifics I had mentioned. She was intent and trusting, and I could lean into her faith. I was so tired and discouraged.

The weeks surrounding the 26th were so much harder than I could have imagined. I'm so thankful that Sue warned me it could be difficult, or I really would have been afraid. As it was, I didn't know how long the pain would last, and that was scary enough. It may be true that the very worst part of the grief is past. I hope so!

A friend's mom said it had been six years since her husband had died and that this year the date had passed without her even being aware. It's not that she's forgotten. I found that hopeful.

Hacking Through
the Jungle

OVERWHELMED MOUNTAIN

I think we ate fast food for months. It was a big step forward when I could decide which "take out" to buy. Making decisions was almost impossible during those first months. Everything was hard: the laundry, dealing with insurance companies, the mail, cleaning, work … it all felt like too much.

Grocery shopping was awful. Now, looking back, it makes sense. For 15 years a huge part of my mom role had included cooking—lots of cooking. Now, abruptly, everything had changed. I still had people to cook for, but my grief so engulfed me that it was painful. I remember pulling into the grocery store parking lot and thinking, "The sun should not be shining because my world has stopped. How can everyone just be going on as though everything is the same?" It would be hard enough to just crawl into a cave and deal with the grief. But the rest of the world insisted on moving forward. I felt removed, as though there were a leper's flashing neon sign on my head that said, "My son died!" Why didn't people see it? I felt so isolated. Grocery shopping was just too normal an activity. I didn't feel normal.

The market was like a minefield for a grieving heart. I just never knew when it would set me off. The macaroni and cheese aisle could be lethal. How many contests had the boys had over who made the very best? Then, too, there were always little boys … sometimes with big brown eyes. Too many things could trigger a memory … too many memories.

And what about the people? Sometimes I just wasn't up to dealing with unexpected encounters. When someone pretended not to see me, were they just in a hurry, or didn't they want to deal with my pain? And when I'd run into someone and they said nothing, did they know? Should I say, "Did you know that Jason died?" Could I handle telling them? What if they did know but just didn't know what to say? Such awkward moments are hard on a good day.

Or what if they did know and did want to help? Being the object of well-intentioned advice can happen anywhere, but my most vivid memory was in the produce aisle. I was trapped for 20 minutes. Someone knew JUST how I felt. Her mother had died when she was 16 and, and, and ... the advice gushed on.

Here's my advice. People do not know how you really feel. But you do. If you find yourself "trapped by good intentions," feeling overwhelmed by unsolicited advice, give yourself permission to exit. Just look at your watch and say, "Oh, look at the time. I need to go." Who wants to wilt in the lettuce aisle?

Be kind to yourself. If you cannot handle cooking today, or laundry, or whatever, it's OK. Do what you can, and leave the rest undone. When you need to hide out for a while, it's OK. If making two decisions wears you out, then give yourself credit for the two you made. Being hard on yourself will not help the healing.

This is the motto I chose to live by:

Whatever I do, I get an "A" for.
Whatever doesn't get done doesn't matter!

Philippians 3:13–14

Brothers, I do not consider myself yet to have taken hold of it. But one thing I do: forgetting what is behind and straining toward what is ahead, I press on toward the goal to win the prize for which God has called me heavenward in Christ Jesus.

Oh Lord, sometimes everything or anything feels like too much. Help me please when I feel like everything is piling up around me. Help me to deal with one thing at a time and not to look at the mound. Help me to prioritize, do my best, and leave the rest to You. Amen.

What is overwhelming you? What's the most important thing you need to do today?

ANGER BOG

The anger bog is a murky, sticky, muddy mess. It churns and consumes. It has no bottom. The edges are semi-soft, but should you be enticed to move into the center, you will find it more like quicksand, and so gooey you will find it hard to extract yourself without help.

As I initially read about grief, I had the most trouble identifying with anger. I see now that for me it was a matter of definition. *Webster's New World Dictionary* defines anger as "a feeling of displeasure resulting from injury, mistreatment, opposition etc., and usually showing itself in a desire to fight back at the supposed cause of this feeling." It goes on with the "SYN—anger is broadly applicable to feelings of resentful or revengeful displeasure." I understood anger as being related to revengeful displeasure. So when I read the stages of grief, I didn't relate to anger because I didn't seek revenge. But did I feel displeasure resulting from injury? Yes! So by the first definition, I was angry!

Anger is a bog! Even in writing this section, feelings of frustration and anger bubble to the surface, leaving me bogged down and frustrated! Today I can recognize it for what it is; back then, I wasn't able to identify anger. To pull apart the fabric of grief and analyze it is like trying to take a piece of paper and return it to its original state ... a tree. The components may be there, but once you've made paper, you can't go back to the tree. To try to separate anger and the other ingredients of grief is to no longer have grief ... just separate, messy emotions. Grief doesn't come in nice clean sheets of paper but all in a muddle ... feelings everywhere. Anger is usually mixed together with other emotions to make a multi-colored page. When I read that anger was part of the process, it didn't make sense to me. Those books were frustrating. Talking about the stages of grief felt too clinical. "Don't treat me like you're dissecting a bug!" I didn't think I was angry because I wasn't mad at anyone or anything in particular, I was just hurting.

But the anger showed: A sunny day was wrong; happy people and normal activities like shopping were "wrong." I wanted the world to stop. I wanted to get off. I didn't want to deal with life without Jason. I hated the sadness, the adjustments and the pain. Daily life was frustrating. I didn't want to have to deal with the realities. I felt much anger because people were ill-informed about the grieving process. As a result, they would judge me or others struggling through the mire. I was angry.

Labeling anger as a component of grief confused me at the time because of my misunderstanding of the definition. Sometimes it's hard to identify. But you don't have to figure it all out. It's not just you, and it's not abnormal if you feel angry, even if it doesn't look like anger.

Hebrews 3:13
But encourage one another daily, as long as it is called today, so that none of you may be hardened by sin's deceitfulness.

Lord, please help me to not be controlled by my emotions. When I'm feeling overwhelmed, help me run to You. When I'm angry, help me to understand and to forgive. Amen.

What makes you want to yell "Help!"?

_____

_____

_____

_____

_____

_____

_____

_____

_____

SORROW SEA

A song, a boy on a bicycle, or a kind word could trigger tears. I just never knew when a fresh batch of wet would run out of my eyes. Sometimes I'd wish there were a trap door in church so I could just drop out of sight and have a good cry.

I think the reason I wanted to cry alone is twofold. I prefer to handle my emotions alone, in my room. The other is that so few people understood the tears. They had thought they caused them, and they felt badly. When I could, I'd try to educate them, but sometimes it was just too much effort. My Tears 101 lecture went something like this, "You didn't cause the tears. The tears are there because I'm in pain. When you 'give me permission' to cry because you've asked about Jason, it's like opening a valve on a pressure cooker. It's good to let the pain out. It's good for me to cry. Sometimes the sorrow just builds up to the boiling point, and I'm not aware. So an opportunity to release the pressure is a gift. Did you know that tears have different chemical properties, depending on what causes them? These are healing tears. It's good to acknowledge my pain. It helps. It's very compassionate, and I appreciate it."

On a good day I could help a friend to understand. Sometimes I just needed to be alone. My favorite place was the little loveseat in our bedroom. I would picture myself in Father God's arms as I sobbed. He would hold me and comfort me. He understood. I didn't need to say a word. Quite often the phone would ring, and someone would say, "You were on my heart and I just wanted to check on you." What a gift it is to have people who listen to the prompting of the Holy Spirit.

Occasionally, I knew I needed to cry, but I couldn't. I could feel the pressure building up but couldn't release it. At those times I found it valuable to try to stimulate them with a sad movie or maybe a song that was meaningful for me.

I got so tired of crying I was sure my tear ducts would dry up for lack of fluid in my body. Crying is not a sign of weakness. It's human. It's part of the healing process.

Early Journal Entry
(About tears and the day of the funeral)

Jesus, I love you! Jason, I miss you!! The tears are good. It's like there are x numbers of tears that need to be shed, and as they're released it is just that—a release and some sense of comfort or peace follows. Almost a sense of well being. So when they get triggered, it's good. People don't like to see you cry— but it's good. Not the poor me, self-centered, heavy kind, but the I'm lonesome, we'll always miss him kind. Thank You, Lord, for showing me in the very beginning the difference between good grief and heaviness. Good grief is when something stirs you—like a huge pan of brownies, making me think, "Oh, Jason would love this." Then I get this wash of happy, sad tears. And I smile at the memory of how much he loved quantities of food. And I'm sad from missing him, and there are tears and release and comfort and peace. But later in the dining room (same day), with people all around and food again before us, I have this heavy feeling. Just morose. It struck me by surprise, and I didn't know what to do with it. The phone rang. Dear friend calling to tell me about an opportunity for her to share the love of Jesus with someone at the grocery store as a result of the funeral. Before we knew it we were praising God for how He was using all of this. Afterward, I noted my marked change of mood. What had caused that? Focusing on Jesus and recalling His works—"Put on the garment of praise for the spirit of heaviness." Then what was that spirit of heaviness?

*Just that—a spirit of heaviness—a not to be grasped or identi-
fied heaviness—foreboding. Worse than fear but closely related.
Definitely not from God. Thank You, Lord, for showing me so
clearly and early the distinct difference between grief and heaviness. For grief there is relief. Tears, sharing, laughing. Heaviness
must be praised away.*

John 11:35
Jesus wept.
(He wasn't alone; people saw him.)

Lord, please hold them. Amen.

How are you doing living life one day at a time?

_____

_____

_____

_____

_____

_____

_____

_____

_____

"The pain is part of the deal.
It proves how much we loved."

THE "Y" ROAD

"Why?" in this context says to me, "If only I could go back and change the outcome of that day." Or, "How am I going to live with this pain?" If there is anything I've learned from this process, it is that looking back and wishing there were something I could do to change things will never accomplish the desired outcome, which would be to bring Jason back. Living one day at a time is the "simple" answer. Certainly not easy.

I didn't go down the "Why?" road. I've watched others do so. It does not change anything. It cannot. There is no happy end to it. It is a waste of time and energy, so I would not go. I'm glad I didn't.

Matthew 6:34

Therefore do not worry about tomorrow, for tomorrow will worry about itself. Each day has enough trouble of its own.

Dear Father, Please help every sad heart to rest in Your loving care, knowing that each person is more valuable than the sparrows You faithfully watch over. Amen.

How can you try to live one day at a time, resting in God's loving care?

NO RULES

There is no right time to go through your loved one's belongings. I felt guilty that I hadn't done it right. What would "right" look like? It's one of those things you muddle through as best you can. Do what you can when you can. Don't condemn yourself for not doing it soon enough or not waiting long enough. Maybe there are those you could bless with some personal things. Maybe it's just too hard in the beginning to deal with.

Going through the drawers and closets was excruciating for me. I still have a little trunk with some of Jason's things, along with a plastic storage box full of cards and notes. I have his sheets in a drawer, as well as a tiny pillow he had since birth. I have his sweatshirt and his spring jacket in case I want to wear something of his. His scuba mask and flippers are under a bed—they were so important to him, and I just didn't know who to give them to.

It's been 15 years, and I know I've healed as much as I am able. It's not that I need those things anymore; I just really don't know what to do with them. Yes, some of these things I might have given away earlier; maybe I still will if the right opportunity arises. But if I never do, they aren't hurting anyone. Be gentle with yourself. There are no rules.

James 1:5

If any of you lacks wisdom, he should ask God, who gives generously to all without finding fault, and it will be given to him.

Dear Lord, sorting through the physical remains of someone we love can feel so final. To part with things they loved or simply touched can feel like losing them all over again. We feel the need to cling to these material reminders of their existence. Help us, Lord, in this very practical step of moving forward in our grief. Amen.

Is there someone you could bless with the things that are not being used?

_____

_____

_____

_____

_____

_____

_____

_____

_____

_____

"Sometimes I feel like a weather
vane and the wind keeps
changing—I've been spinning."

LOST LAKE

My "computer" seemed to have a disconnect virus. I couldn't find names in my brain. I couldn't concentrate. I couldn't make required decisions. I couldn't think clearly. At work I needed to integrate information from customers to orders. There would be calculations to make and sizes to change or verify. I would read customers' letters over and over, but I could not comprehend what was needed. I felt lost.

A year later I was talking to Sarah, a friend whose toddler had died from drowning. She had the same issues. When Sarah's sister, who is a nurse, gave her a medical explanation for it, we both felt better. Since then, I've gotten input from some counselors, and I find the explanation helpful. The grief acts like static on a radio; it comes and goes. It is interference caused by emotions. Normally, when we focus or concentrate, we block out other stimuli, but in deep grief we don't have the ability to block it out. Pain shuts down our other senses, makes it impossible to think.

It's almost like attention deficit related to the incident. The priority in our minds is the reality of the loss. We can't make ourselves focus on something that is not anywhere near as important. Understanding how this pain incapacitated my ability to concentrate and make decisions explains why as I began to heal my ability to turn down the static and function normally returned.

Not being able to concentrate was annoying and frustrating, leaving me feeling scared for my mental health. Understanding that my thought processes were normal under the circumstances helped me not to worry about my lack of concentration.

Psalm 104:33–34
33 I will sing to the LORD all my life;
   I will sing praise to my God as long as I live.
34 May my meditation be pleasing to him,
   as I rejoice in the LORD.

Dear Lord, help those in grief to be patient with themselves as they heal. Help them to trust you. Amen.

Meditating on a meaningful Scripture verse can be very helpful. Try it and record your thoughts.

_____

_____

_____

_____

_____

_____

_____

_____

_____

_____

_____

"When I'm in heavy grief,
decisions are very hard."

AROUND OVERWHELMED MOUNTAIN, AGAIN

Difficult things seem to come in bunches. When they do, dealing with the emotions and decisions can feel overwhelming.

When Wayne's mom died a few months after Jason's accident, I felt as though all the stitches in my grieving heart were ripped out, and I started to emotionally bleed all over again.

There were hundreds of thank-you cards to write, an opportunity to paint a mural for our new children's museum, and I was needed back at work full time. The part-time summer hours they had granted me needed to come to an end. The position was very technical, and I could not concentrate. I couldn't do it all. How very sad to be faced with such difficult decisions when making choices on even a small scale is outrageously difficult. We needed the money, but I chose to come back home, write thank-you notes, take care of my family, and paint the mural at the children's museum in honor of Jason. I had a need for something to feel "normal" again.

Being at home and creating murals was what I had done until about two years before Jason died. At that time we experienced another huge loss. Wayne's 20-year position as a traffic manager for a large paper converter was terminated when there was a company buyout. Because there was nothing else available in his field, his next job left us financially hurting. I went back to office work full time. So for me going "back home" felt good and right. Leaving my job was an option for me because there was insurance money to help tide us over. Not everyone is so fortunate. I didn't have the presence of mind to ask whether there was a position they could put me in that would be less stressful and less responsible until I could heal. I did know that it was too much to try to keep on keeping on. I did know I had some things I needed to do for me.

Was it the best choice? I did the best I could for who I was right then. Even if it wasn't, going back now and asking "What if?" would not help. So, to quote Paul in Philippians 3:13–14,

"Brothers, I do not consider myself yet to have taken hold of it. But one thing I do: Forgetting what is behind and straining toward what is ahead, I press on toward the goal to win the prize for which God has called me heavenward in Christ Jesus."

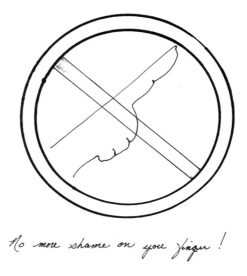

No more shame on you finger !

The "shame on you" finger just does not apply to you.

Romans 8:1
Therefore, there is now no condemnation for those who are in Christ Jesus.

Lord, please help each dear one with guidance in decision making. Amen.

Do you have hard choices to make? Is there someone you trust who can help you look at them objectively? Can you postpone them for a while?

_____

_____

_____

_____

_____

_____

_____

_____

_____

_____

_____

"Grief is like being out of step
with the whole world."

HOLIDAY HOLES

Holidays, birthdays, mealtimes, bedtimes—any time the family was normally together accentuated the huge hole in our lives. Some difficult days I expected, like Christmas. Other days, like my birthday, were especially hard because I hadn't anticipated they would be. How the memories flooded in. Jason had always bought me a Cadbury chocolate-almond candy bar, my favorite. He was such a sentimental kid; the cards he gave were always very sweet. I missed his hugs, his teasing, and his laughter every day. But on those special days, it was worse. The first day of school in the fall caught me off guard, too.

3rd month:

Wish I had forced myself to write those first days. Such a whirlwind of emotions. So tired. Such peace. When I think of how strong, yet how weak, what an amazing time. So comforted, so sad ... On Monday—the first day of school—tears, lots of tears. On my bed crying and crying. Emotions raw again. We had thought Grandma's dying would be like a parenthesis in our grief—we really weren't prepared for it setting us back so. So I'm sobbing. Thinking of the fun first year at the high school, the homecomings, the proms, his friends, all the things that would never be ... Then just so plainly in my mind I hear Jason's voice clearly say, "Yea, right, Mom, like I'm really missing school." And I laughed right out loud and got up and went on with my day. It makes me smile so to think of it. Really, school he would not miss. Erika (his girlfriend), friends, fun, yes, but school—get real.

5th month:

So much to do. I feel overwhelmed. Lord, please take care of Thanksgiving arrangements and decisions. It seems like now I cry many, many times a day. I don't know if that is really any different from what it was. Maybe just the break from it when we were busy with the excitement of Emily's birth [our first grandchild] and the Christmas shopping diversion. Getting back to the reality of the grief is so hard. Maybe I'm not so numb or just the passage of time—the reality of it all. It's so sad. I'm so sad.

I found that the dread I had in advance of holidays was usually worse than the actual day. Somehow the anticipation was worse than the reality. Jesus had something to say about that; "Sufficient unto the day is the worry thereof."

Being aware of the need to be gentle with myself and not be afraid was a tightrope walk. I kept moving forward, but oh so carefully. If I went too quickly, I could take a real fall.

How to handle holidays and anniversaries is, like the rest of grieving, a very personal issue. If only there were a set of rules: This works, but this doesn't. It is still important for me to do something in memory of Jason at Christmas, and I often buy myself a little gift on my birthday from him. On his birthday I still cry; I visit the cemetery, and I pray for friends and family to come to know Christ. I've developed strategies that work for me. There is no right or wrong way to do this. Pray and trust what you think is best for you and your family, knowing that this may need to change from year to year.

Philippians 4:6–7

Don't worry about anything; instead, pray about everything. Tell God what you need, and thank him for all he has done. Then you will experience God's peace, which exceeds anything we can understand. His peace will guard your hearts and minds as you live in Christ Jesus. (NLT)

Dear Lord, please be with these dear ones as they struggle to know how to best handle this difficult time of year. Bless them as they seek meaningful ways to deal with the holiday or anniversary before them. Give them Your peace and direction. Be their comfort and their guide. Amen.

What days are the most difficult for you? Do you need a new plan?

_____

_____

_____

_____

_____

_____

A wise counselor once advised me, "Speak to yourself as sweetly and gently as you would to a tiny, fluffy chick."

THE EXCLUSIVE CLUB

After Jason's death, I found myself a member of a club I had never asked to join. This exclusive group has a costly entrance fee— the death of someone or something you dearly love. The daily dues—grief caused by the severing of a loving relationship. Your companions, Loneliness and Isolation, are continually singing the theme song, "Alone, alone, always alone."

Isolation comes. People don't know how to react to your pain unless they have experienced it. Your pain scares them. It is too raw, too harsh. Friends want to help, but they don't know how. The song continues: "No one understands, alone, alone, always alone," and people avoid you.

Try not to take it personally. Friends want you to be "all better." They want you to be the way you were before. It's impossible. You will be developing a new you, a new normal, a new life. And as long as you try to recover the past, you will not move forward into your new future. These people may or may not be a part of it. Try not to exclude them based on their ignorance or the unintentional hurt that comes as a result.

I found that there was only one Friend who continually understood and was always able to meet me at my deepest level of pain, and that was my heavenly Father. I cried in His arms day after day, and He held me and sang, "Alone, alone, never alone." When I could let Him hold me instead of resenting people who didn't "get it," I was able to experience one incredible gift of grief—His amazing presence.

Jesus said, "Blessed are those who mourn, for they shall be comforted." That comfort, I have found, is more of Him. I come to Him in grief, and He kisses away the pain. He holds me and reassures me that He has a good plan for my life, plans for a future and a hope. "Never, never alone," we sing together.

As I learned to turn to Him in my pain, He helped me to reach out to others and allow them to be part of my healing too. I could express my grief to them and allow them to comfort and encourage me. My life is exclusive no longer; others are invited in to see what Jesus can do to heal a broken heart. Jesus said that he came to heal the brokenhearted. It's true! He did it for me; He will do it for you. You never have to be alone.

Proverbs 23:18
There is surely a future hope for you, and your hope will not be cut off.

Dear Father, thank You that I never was really alone—it just felt that way. It was so hard to be avoided because people didn't know how to reach out and love me in my pain. Thank You that You did. Oh, Lord, please be with my friends today who need to know that You will never, never leave them. Help them to be able to cry in Your arms and receive the incredible comfort of Your love. In Jesus' name, Amen.

Are you isolating yourself?

_____

_____

_____

_____

_____

_____

_____

_____

_____

_____

FINDING A NEW NORMAL

In the beginning my struggle was trying to get my life back to normal. The problem with that effort is that the task is impossible. I could not. There was no way to bring Jason back, and he was a huge part of my normal. At 15, healthy, energetic and intelligent, he touched every facet of my life. To think I could find my way back to normal without him was a search for the impossible.

When I read somewhere that I needed to find a new normal, things started to make sense. What would this new normal look like? I wanted to be happy, live a productive life, have wonderful family times, and know I hadn't wasted the life I'd been given. How to get there? That's been the struggle in my journals. Knowing that the goal is different from what I had thought, having a new paradigm, was a good beginning.

Jeremiah 29:11–13
"'For I know the plans I have for you,' declares the LORD, 'plans to prosper you and not to harm you, plans to give you hope and a future. Then you will call upon me and come and pray to me, and I will listen to you. You will seek me and find me when you seek me with all your heart.'"

Lord, normal sounds so far away. How do I get there? Please, please by my guide. Amen.

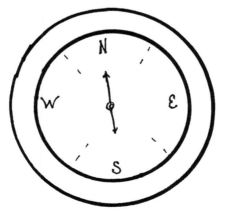

Do you need to change directions?

_____

_____

_____

_____

_____

_____

_____

_____

_____

_____

_____

"The healing process is in
God's hands.
Smile! Lighten up!"

VICTORY ROAD

Dear Ray,

*Thank you for reminding me. If you hadn't been so thoughtful,
I really might have forgotten forever this very significant detail
of the funeral. I appreciate so much your coming to me on that
warm summer day almost a year after the accident. (I would
still rather say "the accident" than the day Jason died.) You told
me about a conversation with your friend at work. You told him
that my smile at the cemetery spoke to you about our faith. I really wasn't aware of everyone who came to the graveside after the
service. Of course you would have been there; your son was one
of the pallbearers. We went to high school together and have been
neighbors for years. Thank you for coming. And thank you for
reminding me that I smiled, because I had forgotten. But when
you told me, I knew exactly when it happened.*

*I can feel it still. The sun was splashing light through the huge
old maple trees. There were flowers and people all around.
Pastor Tom was speaking words that I had heard many times
at open graves. But that day, God's words leaped into my heart,
"This same body will put on immortality." This very same body
that I loved and held, hugged and kissed, will, like Jesus, rise
again. It is true. We will have eternity together. I smiled softly to
the Lord in quiet understanding and thanksgiving. Thank you,
Ray, for reminding me that I smiled.*

Your thoughtfulness brought me much joy.

Your friend and neighbor,
Peg

Romans 8:11

And if the Spirit of him who raised Jesus from the dead is living in you, he who raised Christ from the dead will also give life to your mortal bodies because of his Spirit who lives in you.

Lord, help us to live in the reality of the resurrection. Help us to think of the joyful reunion there will be for us and our loved ones. Amen.

Is there someone to whom you could write a note of thanks for their thoughtfulness?

"Do the next right thing."

DEPRESSION PIT

It didn't get easier. Six months into my grief journey, Christmas was past and the New Year felt anything but happy. There was no comparison between this depression and my normal January blues. It wasn't from the light deficiency so common in the north, and it wasn't the sudden withdrawal from Christmas fudge. I was deeply down. The little love seat in the corner of our bedroom was a constant companion. One day as I lay there all wrapped in an afghan crying out to God, He responded deep within my heart: "Do you remember the funeral?" "Yes, Lord, I remember."

The funeral was on June 30, 1992, and Wayne and I were both filled with anticipation, peace and, yes, joy. Not normal. Definitely not normal. Where was the pain, the fear and the heaviness? My thought was "How can you be looking forward to going to the funeral of Jason and his friend Michael? My deepest heart entreated God, "How can this be?" The answer was instant and profound: "Do you remember the revival you have been praying for? Well, this is the kick-off," He whispered to my heart.

Wayne and I had referred to the funeral as a coronation—the day we celebrated Jason going home to be with the King of Kings and Lord of Lords. Memories flooded over me. There were loved ones hugging on us, a busload of teens from camp singing "Lean on Me," and Pastor R. A. telling everyone their lives could be changed because of the love of Christ. During Jason's favorite song, "The Victory Chant," I had a sense of the parting of the veil between this world and eternity. I "saw" Michael and Jason "high-fiving" each other, right up front, under the suspended cross, because we understood. They're alive! "Yes, Lord ... I remember."

Quickly, softly, sweetly came His gentle reply: "The same power that was available to you then is available to you now. The same Holy Spirit that raised Jesus Christ from the dead is available to you every day." I didn't have to make it on my own. I couldn't. Jesus could and would give me the strength, the grace to live if I would ask and avail myself of His power.

I wish I could say I always chose victory. I didn't. There were many ups and downs. The hardest decision was to live—not just to exist or to tread water until Jesus comes ... but to live, truly live! It was good to remember that Jesus paid for me to enjoy an abundant life. My heart longed for it, and Jason would want me to experience it. It was good to be reminded that the Holy Spirit longs to fill me with His love, joy and peace. On the days I remembered to ask Him, I walked in victory, reminding me now of the words of that song that go "Hail Jesus, you're my king. Your life frees me to sing!" Revival certainly began in my heart.

Romans 8:11

And if the Spirit of him who raised Jesus from the dead is living in you, he who raised Christ from the dead will also give life to your mortal bodies through his Spirit, who lives in you.

Dear Father, I want to pray for anyone struggling with the desire to go on. Please comfort them, Lord, with Your presence and give them the reassurance that You will never leave them nor forsake them. Comfort them now as only You can. Fill them with hope and peace. In Jesus' name, Amen.

Do you need help crawling out of a depression pit?

_____

_____

_____

_____

_____

_____

_____

_____

CLIMBING OUT OF THE PIT ACTIVITIES

These activities helped me:

- Write in a journal
- Call a friend
- Read the Psalms, especially equating the enemy to death
- Go to a grief group
- Watch a sad movie (I didn't feel so all alone.)
- Exercise
- Clean a closet
- Play with the kids
- Go shopping
- Sing to the Lord
- Watch a funny movie
  (A merry heart does good like medicine.)

"Climbing out is not a straight path
up the cliff climb.
It is around and around,
slowly up a widening path
onto firmer ground,
more light, more air, a better view."

"You don't have to do it alone.
The same Holy Spirit who raised Jesus
from the dead is available to you every day.
He will give you life."

ADVICE ABOUT BIG DECISIONS

You aren't yourself. For probably at least two years you aren't thinking logically. Don't make big decisions. Don't change your lifestyle. Don't break up a marriage. Don't break off an engagement. Don't sell your home. Don't remarry. Don't quit a job. And don't take a new job. Give yourself time to heal first. Dream about changes if you like, *but don't do anything permanent yet!*

You just aren't thinking clearly. You may feel compelled to move forward, to do something constructive. STOP! The constructive thing you are doing is healing. That is enough. As best you can, avoid changing your normal way of life. Enough change has taken place; you need time to assimilate the huge effect of the loss. The temptation is to run out and do something, anything to alleviate the pain. You can't. You'll only make it worse.

Advice, of course, is free, and as a result easily ignored. I'm thinking of my friend Sarah, whose toddler drowned in a neighbor's pool. They moved as soon as they could; she couldn't bear seeing that pool every day. Good time to break the rule. There were times when I wanted to move too. Seeing Jason's friends outside broke my heart ... for them and me. I wasn't sure the neighborhood would ever feel like home again. It does. I'm glad we stayed. Good time to heed the advice.

I certainly "broke the rule" when I quit work. I simply felt I could not do it. The work was technical and I couldn't concentrate. I had an opportunity to do something I felt was very meaningful in creating a mural for the local children's museum. It depicted the nine months of a mother's pregnancy with "tummy doors" so the children could "watch the baby grow" when they opened the doors. I used Jason's baby portrait in the final portion where the mommy was holding the baby. I couldn't do that and work. Had they allowed me to take a leave of absence I may not have quit, but I'm not sorry. Financially it was an issue though, and it certainly left me with questions at times.

It would be nice if employers were able to allow leaves or perhaps provide work that is less mentally demanding during the healing process. If this is an issue in your job, ask for what you need. You may be surprised at the compassion offered.

You will get through this. Remember Paul's words in Ephesians 4:13: "I can do everything through Christ who gives me strength" (NLT). Live as normal a life as you can. This will keep you from sinking into despair, and it will give you a purpose for each day. If you need to do something new, volunteer somewhere. There are always people who need you.

James 1:4–6
If any of you lacks wisdom, he should ask God, who gives generously to all without finding fault, and it will be given to him.

Father, thank You. You give advice freely. Help me to seek Your advice and to follow the peace You put in my heart. Amen.

Do you need to stop and reconsider a choice you're about to make?

I HATES

- I hated going to the grocery store.

- I hated having to make decisions.

- I hated not being myself.

- I hated it when people said stupid things. Then I had to deal with the hurt and to forgive them, too, on top of my grief.

- I hated books that tried to dissect grief like a science experiment.

- I hated having to teach my friends about grief. It seemed totally unfair that the patient had to teach the caregivers.

- I hated it when someone would offer unsolicited advice. I felt frustrated, because there was no way I could express my pain, and they didn't understand.

- I hated it that I felt so all alone and misunderstood.

- I hated not having control over my emotions. There was nothing I could do to stop the pain for myself or for the rest of my family.

- I hated being confused about what Jason's doctor had said. It would have been better for me if he had been extremely forthright and clear.

- I hated dealing with insurance companies and money.

- I still hate getting mail addressed to him.

- I still wish he were here.

Ephesians 4:26 (KJV)

"Be angry, and do not sin": do not let the sun go down on your wrath. (NKJV)

Lord, help me to be patient with myself and others. Amen.

What's your favorite thing to hate?

_____

_____

_____

_____

_____

_____

_____

_____

_____

_____

Exodus 14:14
"The LORD will fight for you;
you need only to be still."

FOCUS

Whenever anyone in the family was having a really tough time with the sorrow, one of us would say "Focus," and we all knew what that meant. It wasn't an admonition. It was an encouragement to focus on the truth of the resurrection. As Christians, we believe that Christ conquered death. When He rose again after the crucifixion and then ascended into heaven, He gave believers the promise of eternity with Him and each other. We chose to focus on eternity, the truth of a bigger reality. I love to say, "The truth is that Jesus is alive." Therefore, I can FOCUS on eternity and be comforted.

It was not easy, but it was helpful, positive and imperative to my survival. The Sunday evening after the accident found our little family gathered in the living room with stacks of pictures. We wanted to make a picture collage for the visitation at the funeral home. I was having a really hard time with it, and was standing alone, looking out of the window at the peaceful neighborhood, trying to get a grip on my emotions. Wayne came to me and quietly said, "Focus." He was right. I chose to listen, to heed his advice. I rejoined the family sitting on the floor going through years of family memories. It was not long before the laughter started. It was inevitable because we were searching for meaningful pictures of Jason. He is such a funny guy. There were so many hysterical photos. It was wonderful comic relief. Our laughter floated out of the open windows and doors. Later, our neighbors told us they could hear us and were happy that we could laugh. So am I. We shared stories and memories. We discussed how Jason, mister "I Be Do It!" since he was two, had been first again; first to see heaven.

What a precious memory. The golden thread through the evening and through the days, months and years that follow was the same. Jason is alive with Jesus. This separation is temporary. He would not want to come back here. Jason is just fine.

The center picture was taken just moments before the accident,
and is still my favorite.

He is in heaven and because God loves us, we will be fine too. The love never ends. It is eternal. God is real. Jesus is real. Jesus is alive. Jason is alive. We will all be together again. On these truths I choose to FOCUS.

Philippians 4:8
Finally, brothers, whatever is true, whatever is noble, whatever is right, whatever is pure, whatever is lovely, whatever is admirable—if anything is excellent or praiseworthy—think about such things.

2 Corinthians 10:5
We demolish arguments and every pretension that sets itself up against the knowledge of God, and we take captive every thought to make it obedient to Christ.

Lord, help me to focus on the promise of heaven in the future and in the present on whatever is lovely, admirable and excellent. Amen.

Are you focusing on God's love for you?

_____

_____

_____

_____

_____

_____

_____

COMFORT VALLEY REVISITED

I spent the one-year anniversary week of Jason's death at the camp where the accident had occurred. Kristine and Dan, our daughter and son-in-law, had been counselors at the camp the year before. They wanted very much to go back this year for the returning campers' sake. However, their baby, Emily, needed someone to care for her between feedings. So I (Noni) was elected. What a bittersweet time.

To care for my first grandchild daily in a beautiful north woods setting was very special. To be at the camp where Jason had spent the last days of life just one year earlier was excruciatingly painful. I really sensed, though, that it was the right thing to do. Emily and I took lots of long walks on the wooded paths and looked at the lake, and I cried to the stars. Sometimes the pain was so bad; I didn't think I could stand it. Now, when I look back at that week, I am thankful. I remember the trees and lake, the sun, the kids, and being with Kristine, Dan and Emily.

There were contrasts to the pain, as well as my repeated question, "Why, God, do I have to do such a hard thing?" God had put special people in place to minister to me. One afternoon, on the dock, enjoying the lake, I chatted with the lifeguard. She was from Russia, going to school here in the States. She asked how I happened to be there, and she was so compassionate; it was easy to unburden my heart to her. She gave me two precious gifts that day. One was a little doll, with two tinier ones inside, a memento of Russia and my time at camp. The other was a lighter heart because she was willing to listen. What a wonderful gift.

The other special person was one of the camper's moms. I met her as we were enjoying hamburgers at the big old barn at the end of the week, during a big cookout for all of the campers and staff. She explained that her daughters had been at camp the year before with Jason. Then she gave me the gift of hope. She told me that she had prayed for me every day, all year. God loved me so much that He would have a complete stranger pray for me every day. Incredible! I was so blessed and encouraged. What a healing balm.

There was some unforeseen pain, too. One evening I called home to speak with Wayne, and he had some very disturbing news for me. Paige, a little girl from our church, just 22 months old, had drowned in the neighbor's pool. All I could think of was Sarah, her mother. Paige and Patrick, the twins, were the babies of her active little family. I didn't know Sarah well. We met when she delivered a delicious meal to us after the accident. Sarah was one of those dear people who is just sweet and naturally caring. The time we spent talking was as nourishing and delicious as the plump golden fried chicken she brought. Now, all I could think of was the pain she would be facing.

Walking with Emily that evening, in the fresh pine-scented air, stars speckling the darkness, my heart was breaking for Sarah and crying out to God to take care of her. I prayed for her as another mother had prayed for me. Then there was peace, and I wondered whether Jason was holding Paige.

June 26th, the one-year anniversary of Jason's death, found us at Paige's coronation service. Same church, many of the same people, but especially the same God and the very same peace and comfort.

I knew from the time my children were little that they weren't mine, but God's. It had been a struggle to accept, but I could not live in the fear that something might happen to them. Now, as I reread this journal section and remember that week at camp, this song pulses through my heart: "I'm yours, Lord, everything I am, everything I have, everything I'm not; I'm yours, Lord, try me now and see; see if I can be completely yours."

Can we say with Job, "The Lord giveth and the Lord taketh away, blessed be the name of the Lord"?

Job 1:22 (NAS)
Through all this Job did not sin nor did he blame God.

Oh, Father, for those in the really hard places right now, comfort them, encourage them, and help them to be completely Yours. Amen.

What hard thing do you need God to help you deal with?

_____

_____

_____

_____

_____

_____

_____

_____

_____

_____

_____

_____

James 1:12 (NASB)
"Blessed is a man who perseveres under trial:
for once he has been approved,
he will receive the crown of life, which the Lord
has promised to those who love Him."

WARNING!

"Year two was harder than year one." I hear that from so many people. It's not the pain, because that subsides some. It's the loneliness, the missing them. It's been too long since I've seen or touched him.

Also, everyone else's lives have returned to normal. Mine did not. There were gaps that would never be filled, and I was left to sort out how I could cope with them. This is, of course, how it has to be. But I think I expected to be in a better place. I was better than before, but not totally healed. The struggle of the second year took me by surprise.

Matthew 11:28
Come to me, all you who are weary and burdened, and I will give you rest.

Dear Lord, please help me as I face each new day. Walk beside me and give me strength to face each issue as it arises. Bring healing to my heart, Lord, that I might be able to honestly say, "This is the day the Lord has made, I will rejoice and be glad in it." Only You can bring me to that point, Lord. Help! Amen.

Do **you** *need a day of rest?*

_____

_____

_____

_____

_____

_____

TRAIL NOTES ~ SECOND YEAR

September
13 months

This learning how to function as you begin to heal is … like I've hacked my way through a year of jungle and now the sky is clearer above me, but when I realize moving forward is difficult, I look down to find a thick swamp at my feet—up to my calves and then holes as deep as my chest. In some ways this may be harder. In the jungle there were clearings to lie down in and rest. Ah—but there will be rocks and islands, and I'm closer to shore. Maybe it's just especially hard right here because I've just entered the swamp. "Even though I descend to the pit—Jesus is there." It's just that—right here—it's hard to rest. It's like I have to move because it's too messy to stay in. But I really almost would rather go back to the jungle and rest a bit. I'm so tired and here there's no place to rest. I just need to get to dry land and find a place to rest. It's very uncomfortable.

15 months

Pondering Philippians 3:20 (NASB)—For our citizenship is in heaven, from which also we eagerly wait for a Savior, the Lord Jesus Christ, and Ephesians 2:6–7—And God raised us up with Christ and seated us with Him in the heavenly realms in Christ Jesus, in order that in the coming ages He might show the incomparable riches of His grace, expressed in His kindness to us in Christ Jesus. In some indescribable way we are in Christ. Because Christ is eternal, so am I. Because Christ is seated, so am I. Though now I'm walking here, this is a part of eternity. And in a very real sense what I live matters. Christ in me, the hope of glory. As He is in me, so am I in Him. The life that I now live, I live by faith in the Son of God, who loved me and gave His life for me. Somehow eternity isn't separate from now. We're within eternity—here in this time—and on this earth. Just a glimpse—tiny, tiny. I sense eternity around us here, encompassing us—making our life much more important than we might think. Heaven is not a separate entity in that there is a connection between life here and there—we just can't see it.

16 months

Last night I cried out to God. The mire I felt stuck in was like thick, heavy mud—like all the tears I had cried for Jason in that jungle washed all around and the jungle was an island and the tears saturated the ground and now it was just too heavy to walk through and I was tired, so tired from all the crying and hacking at the jungle and now I'm out and I'm stuck and maybe even if I weren't exhausted I don't know whether I would want to go forward because I don't see anything. It looks hopeless. And that hopeless feeling was because I entertained the thought "What if this is all a lie; how can I go on?" Without Jesus there would be no purpose, and I wasn't sensing Him. Letting go of my confidence in God . . .

I was miserable. Jesus didn't show me a rock to rest on or turn on a light to show me the way. He just picked me right up and said, "Peggy, you're tired; I'll just carry you." Ah, the wonderful peace and rest. It reminds me of that old song, "Love lifted me, Love lifted me, when nothing else would help, Love lifted me." It's true. There was no other way. I was too tired. It was the same choice as the "closet" choice the day after. Are you going to sit down and die or go on? I needed to go on, wanted to, but on my own I couldn't. So He picked me up and I rested—oh blessed rest.

Oh Lord, I'm sorry for doubting You. Holy Spirit, help me to always hear You clearly and keep my vessel clean. Thank You for showing me cracks and weak spots. Lord, I need to do one day at a time ... again! Help me, please. Thank You for holding me and carrying me through the mire.

The pain really does seem to be more contained now ... or at least at present. I don't know that I necessarily have a choice about when it chooses to overcome me. But I'm thankful the last few days have been so much better. I've just really begged the Lord to fill me with His resurrection power. He's so faithful ... "How much more would I give the Holy Spirit to those that ask?"

17 months

I prayed Lord, for Your resurrection power to put life into this body that would rather not go on. Thank You for your faithfulness and Your speedy answer to this prayer. "How much more will I give the Holy Spirit to those that ask." You have made new life surge through me. I can feel it growing and I praise You. Shoots sprouting and leaves beginning to reach out for the sun ... tender and new ... and very much alive. Only You could do that for me.

God showed me so sweetly last night that I need to rest in Him. It's like that picture of Jason at about two with me holding him—we had both fallen asleep. He was so exhausted that he gave up and rested in my arms. Well, I'm that exhausted now. That's what it means—resting in Jesus. Giving up! Just resting ... total love and acceptance from Him, total reliance and surrender from me. Surrender. It's not a negative to surrender fear and grief and anxiety!

18 months

Thank you, Lord, for all You're teaching me—about myself, abut life, about grief. Oh Jesus, the JOY is back!!!

Then I wrote this little song to the tune "My Boyfriend's Back" (an oldie from the 60s)

> My joy's come back and I wanna sing your praises!
> Hey La De Da—My joy's come back!
>
> Jesus came to save and He did the job completely.
> Hey La De Da—My joy's come back!
>
> Circumstances, worry, possessions,
> and people—all try to steal it—
> but my joy's come back!
> Hey La De Da—My joy's come back!

19 months

A gardener said, speaking of his garden, "This is my evangelism, because the beauty points men to God." I'd like my art to point men to God's glory.

20 months

The grieving is different now—where it was a shroud last year, completely encompassing, almost comforting because of its constancy, now it's a dreaded reality. When it steals in and pulls away the progress I've begun to make, it makes me aware of how bad the pain really was last year. Now I want to go forward, I need to somehow, but it's hard, especially after a "slippery spot" because I realize how very fragile I am. I'm lonesome and I need to curl up in Jesus' arms.

Today's the day I baby myself in bed with tea, my Bible and a book. I'm not very in tune with my insides, and that is OK.

To be a little more diverse was part of the plan—less painful to be more outwardly focused now that I can. But when the pain overtakes, as it can sometimes, I'm not only caught off guard, but am almost a little frightened by it. Like maybe I'm not being honest about my pain. I'm not trying to deny that there is pain, but am I doing something wrong when I hurt so badly? I've been pushing too hard. This gift of today that I've given myself is wonderful. I think I should have more compassion for me—just carry on but be gentle.

21 months

I do see improvement. Mostly, I cook meals and do keep up with the laundry and cleaning. At first we were lucky if I could choose the fast food to pick up.

Jason did not die because you were at the office—because you weren't painting. Let that sink in. You cannot blame yourself. There is no answer to why. Not here. Not now. Except that there will be good. What happened was not good, but there will be good.

End of 2nd year

I'm hoping I'll reach a point where I can think of Jason and smile because of how dear he is and not feel sad because he's not here. But I'm thankful that I'm through the worst of that awful grieving jungle. There are long distances now between the periods of intense pain. So when it comes, it is not welcome. (I think there were times when it was welcome; I needed to mourn, I needed to cry, and it was more comfortable to stay in that grieving place than to move forward.) I think I'll change my mind about avoiding the painful days—I need to welcome them, not dread them. It's part of the process too. After all, I've been through much worse. A day or two is nothing compared to two years. They can be a good reality check—Am I living my days, the good days, to the fullest? Am I eternally focused?

Isn't that life—to accept the days as they come? We just aren't in control. All the more reason to order what we can, as in that good old serenity prayer: Oh Lord, grant me the serenity to accept the things I cannot change; the courage to change the things I can; and the wisdom to know the difference.

Yesterday when I talked to _____ about painting and shared with her some of my life, I ran into the same thing I do so often. When I share about You, Lord, and how I could not have made it without You, the standard response is, "Oh, you <u>need</u> that." Yes, yes I do! But so do they. And you are not a <u>that</u>. It isn't "religion"; it's You. If my faith were based on a lie, then I'd be a fool if it helped. On the other hand, since it isn't, since it's based on fact and on Your faithfulness—they're deceived for not seeing that this isn't some little fairy tale I crawl into to make myself feel better. How can I respond, Lord, to that kind of reaction? I want so badly to shine a little light into the situation. I want to shine a lot in! Challenge their preconceived notion that Christianity is a nice crutch for "you." "Glad it works for you." "You need that." They're not putting me down; they're building a wall against the truth for themselves. They quickly brush off my testimony as something I "need." They think it's like I put on salve or something. If salve had no healing power, no one would use it. You'd be dumb even to rub it on. If my faith isn't based in fact and truth, then I'm dumb and it won't heal me. But You do heal me. Father, please help us to harvest quickly. I see the time coming so quickly to an end. Father, thank You for Your spirit and the river of living water that flows through me from You.

Others on the Path

Family and Friends

THE BEDROOM DILEMMA

There were so many things to try to come to grips with all at once. Our varying needs as individuals certainly intensified the stress. Andy and Jason had shared the big dorm room over the garage. It was a great place for boys. You could close the door and almost never hear the noise downstairs. Now the lack of noise was almost insufferable. Jason had been our agitator. When he had entered a room, there would soon be activity, noise, fun, fighting, or any combination of the above. To suddenly be in such silence was a huge adjustment for all of us. Our busy four-child household had seemingly overnight been reduced to one. Kristine had only been married three years and Michelle was a sophomore at college. Andy, alone now, was entering junior high in the fall.

During those blurred early weeks there are some things that leap out. One was the knife-like pain in my chest every time I went into Jason and Andy's room. There was something about Jason's bed tucked under the window with the blue quilt I had sewn for each of the boys. The bed was in an alcove, so when I walked in to put Andy's laundry away, or to kiss him goodnight, I'd almost be caught off guard by the empty bed waiting there in the corner.

Entering their room flooded me with memories. Jason had been so proud of that room. He took great delight in hanging sports posters everywhere. When he and Andy took over the room after Kristine's marriage, I had to curtail his excitement a little, or he would have used all the wall space. I managed to save Andy about six feet, thinking, "Well, when Jason goes off to school, it'll be Andy's turn."

The memories and emotions this room stirred up felt unbearable. I was driven almost wild with grief at the sight of its sameness, and Andy didn't want to touch a thing. When I could handle it no longer, I used the one opening I had to negotiate some change. The carpet really needed to be replaced. In fact, we had purchased it before the accident. So Andy and I finally talked about the need to get the carpet installed. He was OK with that but didn't want to touch the walls. I could handle that. So we compromised. When it came time to put the furniture back in, I suggested that we arrange the furniture in a way that would function better for him. Oh, how thankful I was to get that bed out of the corner. I wanted to stop crying on top of that blue quilt. New bedspreads and a new arrangement really did help. The walls were left the same for Andy.

We were fortunate. I'm so thankful I knew how Andy felt about changing the room. What would have happened if I hadn't known? I might have just torn the whole room apart, changed everything and made his adjustment in HIS room that much more difficult.

I include this story because a counselor told me a very sad story of a marriage ending in divorce because the husband couldn't handle the child's room remaining the same. He totally emptied the room of all signs of the little girl, painted the walls and rearranged the furniture. When his wife returned and saw the room, she was overcome with grief.

Communicating with each other on the hard things, instead of assuming that everyone deals with the loss in the same way, can avoid a lot of pain and frustration. Because we experience things differently doesn't mean we don't care about the deceased. It doesn't mean we are heartless or insensitive. It just means we process differently.

Proverbs 18:21 (NKJV)
Death and life are in the power of the tongue,
And those who love it will eat its fruit.

Oh Father, help us to be sensitive to each other's needs. We are all so different. Help us find a way to get through the pain without further hurting each other. Amen.

Are there some changes you'd like to make, or someone you need to talk with about the problem?

_____

_____

_____

_____

_____

_____

_____

Advice: Talk to each other before you make changes.

Reflections

Mirror still, reflections pure.
A ripple brings distortion.
The likeness disrupted,
Beauty remains.
Calmness returns perfection.

Reflections
Original Oil 24" x 18"

REGRETS

I love to walk around the little lake where we have a summer cabin. It's a great place to exercise my thoughts. One particularly lovely summer day I was plagued with sad thoughts about our Michelle. She had just completed her freshman year at college the summer Jason died. One of the many decisions that needed to be made was whether or not she would go back to school in the fall. The only reason it was an issue was the distance. She attended Asbury College in Kentucky, a good day's drive from Wisconsin, too far to come home except for holidays. We didn't have much time to decide, with school beginning in August. The thought process as I recall went something like this: There's no way to get registered somewhere closer before the beginning of the semester, she has a good group of friends there that will stand by her, if she drops out she may not ever go back to school, and what would she do if she didn't go back? The pros, of course, were that we wanted her with us; we wanted our entire family close by. I'm not sure who made the final decision, but it did seem best for her to go back to school, and that is what she did.

So why the struggle now, years later? Because the one thing we could not have foreseen was how difficult it would be for her to come home. At school she could separate from her grief. She got straight A's. She worked hard and was involved with activities. When she came home … grief was waiting. What a stark reality for her, that quiet house that had once swirled with activity. We who were home had to face his death every day. It was difficult, of course, but we were forced to grieve—and as a result, to heal.

There were many circumstances she suffered through as a result of the decision to return to school. Then, of course, all of my shortcomings as a mom came tumbling into my heart as well. This was getting to be a difficult walk.

Then it struck me. Yet another opportunity to forget those things that are behind and to reach forward. Playing and replaying the tapes of what was, what could have been, what should have been, was useless. I made a decision to draw a line in the sand (well, on the blacktop road) and cross over it, never to look back. Looking back is such a waste of energy. I needed to focus on the future and how to love her and the rest of my family now. So I drew the line, purposed in my heart not to look back, and took a step.

It didn't change the past, but I know it's the right step for our future.

Psalm 35:10 (NASB)
All my bones will say, "LORD, who is like You,
Who delivers the afflicted from him who is too strong for him,
And the afflicted and the needy from him who robs him?"

Dear Father, help these dear ones to let go of the things that lie behind and to press forward. Help them to lean into the future. Help them to trust You to work things out for the good. Help them to focus on what they have, not on what's been taken from them. Help them to be a blessing to everyone around them. May Your peace surround them as they let go of the past. Amen.

Do you need to draw a line?

_____

_____

_____

_____

_____

"Christians grieve differently,
but they do grieve."

THE 80% TALK

Normally, Wayne and I like to take walks together. But this cold winters night I went alone, frustrated. I was glad peoples' windows were closed so that I could vent. I felt so unloved and angry! Being emotionally disconnected from Wayne heaped more pain on my already broken heart. Wasn't it bad enough to lose Jason? Now I felt as though our marriage would surely fracture, too. The statistics would bear out my fear; 80% of marriages that suffer the death of a child end in divorce. I know God heard my cry. He spoke to my pain: "Look at the moon." The clouds blocked it from view. "Does that mean it isn't there?" He asked. "No," I replied. Then he gave me words to cling to: "That's how it is with Wayne's love right now. You can't see it, but it's there."

Another day, we lay on top of our comfy four-poster bed, and I confronted my fear. I told him what I'd learned about the 80% factor. The lies swimming in my mind said I would be better off alone; the pain was too much. Nothing would ever change; I needed to quit. "A divorce would make things easier." After talking and crying, we decided it boiled down to recommitting ourselves to each other. Wayne said, "There will be no divorce."

I agreed. We needed to hear and say the words. We didn't need any more pain, grief or destruction, and neither did our children.

For me, this was like closing all the doors and windows of "escape." It left me with choices of how to best carry on. If I was going to stay in this marriage, and I was, then was I going to be happy or sad? Happy

Shut all the doors & windows...

Keep the love!

seemed wisest. How would I accomplish that? I had no control over Wayne, or of how he was progressing with his grief. I really needed to leave him alone to get through this in his own way. He couldn't help me either. With raw nerves exposed, sensitive to every little stimulus, we desperately needed to heal.

So how was I going to cope? My journal is full of my circling around this issue. It was a lie that I would be better off alone, that somehow if I were alone it wouldn't hurt so much. The truth was that we were better off loving each other and that this was an excellent time to improve our marriage. Love is a decision, an action verb. In the beginning, I could only love myself. God's Word affirmed this: "Love your neighbor as you love yourself." I needed to treat myself tenderly. I cried in Jesus' arms, clung to the psalms, wrote in my journal, rocked my granddaughter, painted, and read books by other parents. I needed to soak in God's supernatural love for me and then open myself to love and respect Wayne through the power of the Holy Spirit. I needed to share the love of Jesus. I needed to stay committed to my family. I did the things I needed to do for me. The Bible says that love is patient, kind, longsuffering, bears no evil, believes all things, hopes all things, and is not easily provoked. I needed to apply this love and gentle nurture to myself. I tried to speak softly to myself as I would to a small child. Slowly, slowly, there were some green shoots of hope poking their way through the icy snow of my pain.

Summer came. As Wayne and I walked together down the familiar tree-lined street, sunshine reflected the warmth of our love. "How is the grief for you?" I asked. He responded, "I feel like I'm crawling up a hill of broken glass on my bare hands and knees." That picture stirred my heart with compassion for his pain. Sometimes we feel we are alone in our misery because we don't hear the other person saying the words. Then I told him how I felt. "It's like I'm in a gigantic jungle. Each day I get out my machete and hack away at the vines impeding my way, only to awaken every morning and discover that the jungle has grown up all about me again. I have to go through it, there is no way around, but which way am I supposed to go?" I felt exhausted, lonely, and frightened.

Communicating our pain when we weren't feeling overwhelmed by it was a positive step. Certainly the differences in our processing styles made our journey more difficult. He sifts and sorts internally and expresses himself in a clean, concise manner. I process and reprocess verbally. During my quiet time, the Lord would often encourage me with Jeremiah 29:11: "For I know the plans I have for you," declares the LORD, "plans to prosper you and not to harm you, plans to give you hope and a future." On bad days I'd repeat it over and over.

The supernatural love we both needed for each other was available through the power of the Holy Spirit. Did we always avail ourselves of it? NO! But because we were committed to our marriage, God's grace overcame the statistics. We are called to be conduits of Christ's love. We tried. The goal was to be able to walk together on the other side of the grief, regardless of whether or not we walked the same path at the same time. It was not easy. It was often frightening and painful.

Reassuring each other of our commitment was a key issue in walking out of the valley hand in hand. Our marriage and intact love have been worth the struggle.

1 Corinthians 13:4–7 (NLT)

Love is patient and kind. Love is not jealous or boastful or proud or rude. It does not demand its own way. It is not irritable, and it keeps no record of being wronged. It does not rejoice about injustice but rejoices whenever the truth wins out. Love never gives up, never loses faith, is always hopeful, and endures through every circumstance.

Dear heavenly Father, my heart aches for those struggling to deal with grief and marriage issues. It can feel so overwhelming. Don't let them be overcome with the lies, but help them walk in the truth of Your love every day. Wrap them in Your love for them, and fill them with Your love and respect for each other. Thank You, Lord. You are so good. Amen.

Your marriage is worth the commitment to walk in love. What do you need to do?

_____

_____

_____

_____

_____

_____

_____

_____

_____

_____

LIFE

Self Discipline

Proverbs 6:
Discipline is the way to life

THE GLASS MOUNTAIN

Communicating was difficult for us, partly because of the pain and partly because of who we are. Wayne processes internally, sifting and sorting, mulling and analyzing all on his own. I read and study, think and pray, but I need to sift through the information verbally in order to come to conclusions. Can you see the conflict here? He would give me a one-liner, and I would give him more information than anyone ever needed to hear. But we kept on plugging away at staying connected as best we could.

The stark contrast between his style of processing and mine was overcome with word pictures. When he could tell me his pain was like crawling up a mountain of broken glass on his hands and knees, I knew we had the same pain. He did understand; he just didn't tell me about every cut and every inch of progress. I, thankfully for him, didn't tell him all of mine either. My journal served as an excellent place to "think out loud." I vented my pain and sorrow on those white pages instead of on Wayne.

In retrospect, that was a good choice. We were both free to circle our own mountains in our own way in our own time. We did the work, God did the healing, and today we are happy and together.

Ephesians 4:2–3

Be completely humble and gentle; be patient, bearing with one another in love. Make every effort to keep the unity of the Spirit through the bond of peace.

Lord, give me grace. Amen.

Because Jesus loves you, you can show your love to _____ by:

_____

_____

_____

_____

_____

_____

_____

_____

_____

"I must confess to a feeling of profound
humility in the presence of a universe which
transcends us at almost every point.
I feel like a child who while playing by the
seashore has found a few bright colored shells
and a few pebbles while the whole vast ocean
of truth stretches out almost untouched and
unruffled before my eager fingers."
–Sir Isaac Newton

"YOU TANT TAY TUPID!"

"You tant tay tupid!" my three-year-old granddaughter used to say. She was the vocabulary police. Too bad we as adults really do say stupid things.

How many "stupid" things have people said to you? Does it help to know that they don't mean to hurt you and that they're trying to help? Or does it feel better to just assume they are insensitive?

Oh, the temptation to list them all right here!!!

It helped me to forgive them immediately. Otherwise I would have had to carry around the guilt of unforgiveness along with the hurt feelings … too heavy a load.

1 Chronicles 21:8
Then David said to God, "I have sinned greatly by doing this. Now, I beg you, take away the guilt of your servant. I have done a very foolish thing."

Father I forgive _____ *for their hurtful words. Amen.*

Will you let go of the pain inflicted by thoughtless words?

_____

_____

_____

_____

_____

_____

_____

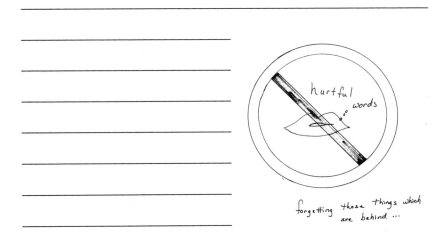

ISOLATION—THE SILENT KILLER

While it may seem easier to stay away from the world because "no one understands," that is a tactical error. The Word says that our adversary the devil goes about seeking whom he may devour. A sheep all alone is prey to the wolves. Find a counselor, a friend, a relative who is patient and supportive, and lean into them when it's too much to go it alone.

1 Peter 5:8
Be self-controlled and alert. Your enemy the devil prowls around like a roaring lion looking for someone to devour.

Father, when we're weak You're strong. We need You to help us be vigilant. Protect us, Lord, from all evil. Amen.

Do you need to call a friend or a counselor?

_____

_____

_____

_____

_____

_____

_____

_____

_____

PERMISSION

If a woman's husband dies, she is a widow. If a man's wife dies, he is a widower. When a child dies, there is no word for the parent. In social settings, this can result in a situation worse than awkward. In fact, for me there was one question that could strike panic. "How many children do you have?" It's an innocent query, often asked in a setting that has nothing to do with grief. But it could leave me feeling frozen, confused, and frustrated.

I remember the dilemma all too well. What was I to say? If I answered "Four," they would assume four living children. What if they asked more questions; that could lead me to talking about things I may not want to discuss. If I said "Three," it's like I'm denying Jason as our son. Awful! He is and always will be our son. This may sound trivial or inconsequential to someone who has not experienced such a loss, but it cuts to the core of the pain. Our child is no longer here. It is amazing how often the question is asked. It's a very typical small talk kind of inquiry. "Where do you work? Where do you live? How many children do you have?" It's the normalcy that is so disarming—that and the feeling of being caught off guard, a little ambushed when it happens. "Oh, I wasn't thinking I'd have to deal with this topic in this setting. It wasn't on my mind and now it is." Or, "It is constantly on my mind and I dread dealing with it in social settings."

So first of all, if you've lost a child, you are not abnormal if this is a troublesome issue. If your loss is a brother, sister, parent, or spouse, there may be other questions that make you cringe. Having a ready response helped me. I would answer honestly, "Four." I had a stock answer. I would say each child's name in order. "Kristine is the oldest and lives in town with her family, etc. Michelle lives in Point and loves her job, Jason has gone to be with Jesus, and Andy lives in Appleton with a couple of guys from college." I had it all worked out ahead of time so I didn't have to stumble around for words. I acknowledged my need to still claim him as an important part of our family. I solved any awkward silence by having something to say. I hope this helps. I mostly wanted to give you permission to continue claiming your loved ones!

Psalm 127:3
Sons are a heritage from the LORD, children a reward from him.

1 Corinthians 15:20–22
But Christ has indeed been raised from the dead, the firstfruits of those who have fallen asleep. For since death came through a man, the resurrection of the dead comes also through a man. For as in Adam all die, so in Christ all will be made alive.

Dear Father, thank You for our loved one and the time we had together here. Please help me not to be overcome by the unexpected. Amen.

Are there questions or situations for which you could prepare ahead?

_____

_____

_____

_____

_____

_____

_____

_____

FRIENDS

Some friends seemed to have an intuitive sense of what to do. They weren't afraid to be near me. They weren't afraid to listen. They seemed able to look past the pain and still be my friend. They didn't have expectations for me to change. They listened, prayed for me, and prayed with me. Some even brought meals way past the two-week mark. The Holy Spirit seemed to have some people ready to minister at the slightest whisper; then they would call just when I was desperate.

Some friendships were strained. This was terribly difficult to deal with. It wasn't their fault, of course. They hadn't experienced such intense grief. My pain scared them. They loved me and didn't want to hurt me. If I cried, they felt they had caused my pain. Then I felt obliged to give them my Tears 101 lecture, but sometimes I was just too tired to educate.

Some friends would avoid the subject. Unknowingly, they caused more frustration because I needed to talk. I needed to process, needed an outlet. And because I cared for them and our friendship, I didn't want to be the one to always bring it up.

Communicating was difficult because everything else felt so trite. Nothing held a candle in comparison to the depth of my loss. How could I ever again discuss decorating or the petty squabbles of other children? It put a huge strain on my friendships. Two of my dear friends determined to get me out of the house and tried to take me to lunch on a regular basis. It didn't work out very well for a number of reasons. First, it was too soon for me to get past my pain enough to be interested in anything that seemed trivial, and most things did. Then I had to deal with another issue: Either make the effort to forgive them for unintentionally causing more pain, or stay hurt. It did feel easier sometimes to isolate.

I taught them about the tears when I could. I explained that they didn't cause them but were a catalyst to help release them. How could they know if I didn't tell them that talking about Jason was good therapy for me? How could they know that I wanted to hear stories about him? How could they know how much it hurt to see their children well and healthy when mine was no longer here? They couldn't, and there were no words to express it. But not being with them wasn't the answer either. I had to press past the pain or lose my friends.

I still am probably too intense. Making small talk gets old for me very quickly. I like to talk about deeper things, things that matter for eternity. Heaven seems closer for me now.

It seemed to work best for me if I cried to God and let Him send me the help I needed. It was too hard to reach out. I am blessed: Most of our friendships survived the trauma ... but it wasn't always easy.

Proverbs 13:14 (NLT)
The instruction of the wise is like a life giving fountain; those who accept it avoid the snare of death.

Dear Lord, thank You for being a friend who is always there, always understands the pain and never judges or criticizes. Thank You for Your loving arms that held me. Please hold this dear one right now; please comfort and caress away the pain. Amen.

Are you struggling with a friend or a loved one? Do you need to tell them how you're feeling?

_____

_____

_____

_____

_____

_____

_____

LETTER TO FRIENDS

Do you have some friends or family you need to write to? Maybe what you need to say is best left in your journal. It can be a wonderful release to write from your heart whether you mail it or not. If the letter on the following page fits your needs, feel free to copy and mail it, or just tear it out of the book!

2 Timothy 2:22b (NLT)
… pursue righteous living, faithfulness, love, and peace. Enjoy the companionship of those who call on the Lord with pure hearts.

Oh Lord, sometimes communicating with those we love is the hardest thing. Please help! Give us the words we need to convey our hearts and help us to always seek peace. Thank You for Your loving example of forgiveness. Help us all to walk there too. Amen.

Do you need to write to someone? Why?

_____

_____

_____

_____

_____

_____

_____

_____

_____

Dear friends,

Here are some things I need you to know. I love you, and I want to be with you, but sometimes the typical conversations leave me frustrated and exhausted. Somehow nothing seems important anymore. I can't focus on small talk for long, and the things we had in common before seem trite. I need to talk about my loss but don't want to be the one to bring it up. I need to hear my loved one's name mentioned by someone besides me. I love to hear stories about him. I worry that I may never be able to carry on a normal conversation again. I want you to understand that when you talk about him, it blesses me. Sometimes it may make me cry, but it's good, because I need to. The pressure and pain build up inside like a pressure cooker, and when you, in kindness, ask how I'm doing, or say you miss him too, it gives me permission to accesses my pain in a good way. Crying helps relieve the tension. Please don't be afraid of my tears. They are healing, and you didn't cause them; you helped release them.

I'm looking forward to being "myself" again someday. But I know I'll never be the same. This pain is developing a whole new dimension of me, and it's scary to me sometimes. I need to believe you'll hang in here with me while I struggle through. I love you dearly. Here are the things you can do to help. Just offer, "I want to help. Can I go to the store for you or do your laundry for you?" Make it specific because I don't like to be a bother. Call me for lunch or dinner, but be sure you give me time to talk about the real issues I'm facing. I know this may not be pleasant dinner conversation for you, but it is a huge gift to me to know you care that much.

I'm sorry I'm such a downer. Please be patient with me. I don't want to lose you too.

Your tearful friend,

Lake Helen
Original Oil 16" x 12"

SEA OF GOLD

In the depths of my despair,
Wracked with pain I could not bear,
My Savior, Lord, and friend did meet me.
He held my hand,
He healed my heart,
He set my feet on solid ground.
As I look back,
I feel His kiss upon my head,
His hands upon my shoulders.
We made it.
I will sit here sometimes, I think,
and look back upon that sea of gold
When my Savior and I were melded into one.
I do not comprehend how He could make it so,
My Savior and my friend.

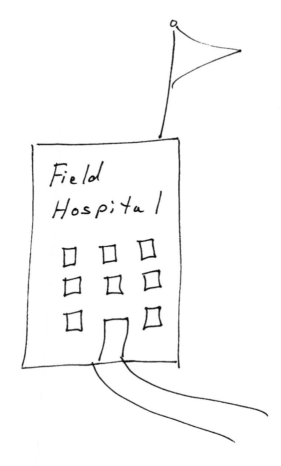

Field Hospital

FAMILIAR PATHS

After speaking with grief counselors and many who have suffered loss, these things appear to be quite common:

- Times and dates, especially in the beginning, can be very difficult:
  Anniversaries of the accident were always unwieldy. In the beginning, every Friday was hard, every day about 12:30 p.m., every 26th of the month. The grief was so in my face that everything reminded me.

- Their smell is important:
  I kept his little pillow because he always slept with it.

- You miss their touch:
  Sometimes I wore his basketball sweatshirt just to feel close to him.

- Pictures may be difficult to deal with:
  I couldn't stand to look at pictures. (Some people want lots of pictures around and need to be careful not to build a shrine.)

- Dealing with their rooms can be a problem:
  I was depressed at the sight of his empty room with everything left just as it was. (Some people need to leave everything the same for a while.)

- Selecting just the right memorial was very difficult.

- When people avoided the mention of his name, I felt sad.

- When people avoided talking about our loss, I felt sad.

It helped me when I realized these things were quite normal. Now I understand, but in the beginning I didn't, so some of these issues made me feel quite crazy.

1 Corinthians 10:13

No temptation has seized you except what is common to man. And God is faithful; he will not let you be tempted beyond what you can bear. But when you are tempted, he will also provide a way out so that you can stand up under it.

Father, would You please hold this dear one in your arms today. Answer their questions, comfort their fears, and guide them as they continue to walk this path. Amen.

Does it help to know that someone else has been this way before and survived?

_____

_____

_____

_____

_____

_____

_____

_____

_____

THE FOUR TASKS OF MOURNING

These were taken from a sheet we received in our grief group. I think they are helpful and accurate.

1. To accept the reality of the loss.
2. To experience the pain of grief.
3. To adjust to an environment in which the loved one is missing.
4. To withdraw emotional energy and reinvest it in another relationship(s).

I'm sorry I don't know the source.

Now I can say from the heart...

Every day is a gift!

AN ALARMING TREND

I often heard people saying it was OK to be angry with God. This alarms me. I can understand being honest with Him about our feelings. I also understand that God can handle our anger. Of course He can. From my perspective, God was the only One who really understood my heart. He was the only One I could really cling to. I was never mad at God, the notion that I should have been seemed ludicrous, the encouragement for others to adopt that mode foolhardy. How much comfort can you receive from someone if you are mad at Him? It would be like a two-year-old child tripping over a tree root, falling down, and getting hurt. He's bloody and crying. His daddy is standing right there, ready to clean the wound, then hold him, caress him, and keep him safe. But rather than accept those comforts, the child not seeing the tree roots that he stumbled over, blames his dad instead. God is lovingly waiting to comfort, but if we are angry with Him how do we receive the love?

God is not to blame for Jason's death. I feel as though I have to defend my Dad. I get so tired of God getting the blame for everything bad that happens on this Earth. He comes to give life abundantly. The enemy comes to kill, steal and destroy. If I'm going to blame anyone, it'll be Satan, not God. I know that God is sovereign and that He could have stopped the accident. He chose not to. I don't question God on this. He is the Master of the universe. He has chosen to give us free will. That's why death exists, because we have the ability to choose. Adam and Eve chose to listen to the enemy and believe that God was trying to keep us from experiencing all we could. Satan lied. He's always lying. I'll bet he lied to our boys that day. "It'll be fun. What difference does it make? You'll be right back. Just a quick spin in the car, come on. Have a little fun. Who will it hurt?" The enemy is always going around like a roaring lion, seeking whom he can devour. Then God gets blamed for our bad choices. But God in His lovingkindness will turn even the worst nightmare into good for those who love Him. I choose to believe He is good. I also choose to believe that because He loves me, He will take care of me. He understands the pain. His Son died too. He promises to comfort those who mourn.

Matthew 5:4
Blessed are those that mourn for they will be comforted.

Dear Lord, for those who are struggling with anger at You, I pray that You will open their eyes to Your compassionate love for them. I pray that they will allow You to hold them and heal them. Amen.

Do you need to let God comfort you?

_____

_____

_____

_____

_____

_____

_____

_____

_____

Lt. Shane Osborne about his
POW experience:
"Prayer, in the end, was the
greatest survival skill I knew."

DON'T ANESTHETIZE THE PAIN

The first day a friend called the doctor for me and ordered sleeping pills. I never took them. My experience with people anesthetizing their pain put a healthy fear of alcohol or drugs before me. As a child, I watched lives being wasted because of alcohol and its effect on family and friends. As a result, I never considered taking drugs.

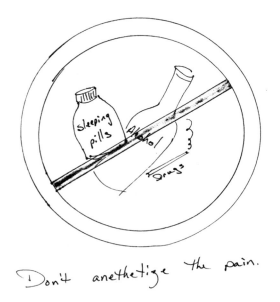

Don't anethetize the pain.

My experience tells me that pills, alcohol, or drugs will only postpone the pain, not obliterate it. You cannot ignore or avoid it. You have to go through it. If you are desperate, get help. Go to your doctor, call a counselor, or speak to your pastor. (Follow your doctor's advice if there is chemical depression.) Find a grief group. There is no glory in "going it alone." As Christians, we are part of a family, a body. Let others help.

1 Corinthians 12:26
If one part suffers, every part suffers with it.

Father, when I am in need of encouragement, help me to turn to You and Your people. Then, Lord, I pray that they will respond according to Your Word and be willing to support me in prayer and friendship. Amen.

Are you looking in the right places for help?

_____

_____

_____

_____

_____

_____

_____

_____

_____

"Spending time with Jesus daily
is not a nice choice;
it is a necessity."

DEPRESSION IS PART OF THE DEAL

Depression is not an indication that you are doing something wrong or that you lack faith; it's just part of the healing process. You may have one or more of these symptoms:

- Anger
- Sleeplessness or the desire to sleep all the time
- Lack of appetite or the desire to overeat
- Mood swings
- Needing to cry for no apparent reason
- Uninterested in things you normally enjoy
- No desire to go anywhere
- Normal activities (like taking a shower) require too much effort.

If these symptoms persist, you may need to see a physician to make sure you aren't chemically depressed. Sometimes medication may be necessary to help put your body back on track.

There is no shame in taking care of yourself. Remember that your body heals when you rest, so a little extra sleep might help.

Psalm 37:39
The salvation of the righteous comes from the LORD; he is their stronghold in time of trouble.

Lord, please help me to heal physically, mentally and emotionally. Amen.

What do you need to do for you today?

_____

_____

_____

_____

_____

_____

_____

_____

In the beginning
pain is all over
the place

Later, it
will be contained...
not so overwhelming

COMING TO TERMS WITH BIG QUESTIONS

It's easy to blame God. After all, isn't He in charge of everything? Couldn't He have made it all turn out differently? And why did this have to happen, anyway, if He's a God of love?

All fair questions. This is how I came to terms with it. Yes, God is in charge. Yes, He could have made it turn out differently. But since He is a good and loving God, I tried to see it from His perspective. He gave us free will, and with that comes the potential for mistakes, poor choices, and in some cases evil people doing dreadful things. Regardless of the cause, the principle is the same. God either has to allow for free choice or not. He does. Therefore, there was a horrible accident that He allowed. Since He allowed it, and He is good, how does that work out for me?

He loves Jason, and Jason is just fine with Him. He's safe, and he's loved. And, what about my pain? If I can go to Him, this God of all comfort, and allow Him to hold me and speak peace to my heart, there will be peace. He holds me. He loves me. He comforts me and consoles me. He blesses me, and He gives me peace. He longs to do that for all who are weary and heavy laden. He is the God of all comfort.

Jeremiah 29:11–13

"For I know the plans I have for you," declares the LORD, "plans to prosper you and not to harm you, plans to give you hope and a future. Then you will call upon me and come and pray to me, and I will listen to you. You will seek me and find me when you seek me with all your heart."

Father, help. Amen.

What issues do you need to wrestle with?

_____

_____

_____

_____

_____

_____

_____

_____

_____

"I need to put on my gospel
armor daily—to walk and
fight the good fight.
Hup two, three, four!"

REBUILDING

Part of what made rebuilding my life so difficult was the intense awareness of things that needed to change. Status quo would not do. So besides trying to pick up the pieces that were valuable but had been blown all over the place, I was trying to build an entirely different structure, one that could withstand the gale force winds of tragedy.

The building took place in the Word of God and under His sheltering wings. Knowing beyond anything else that He loves me and will always comfort and keep me is my strength and my high tower.

Getting rid of old patterns of thinking, learning to confront, learning to trust, learning to pray—these were all part of the mental restructuring that needed to take place. I'm still under construction, but the clutter has been cleared away. The building is much better directed ... like following a good blueprint.

Matthew 7:24–25

"Therefore everyone who hears these words of mine and puts them into practice is like a wise man who built his house on the rock. The rain came down, the streams rose, and the winds blew and beat against that house; yet it did not fall, because it had its foundation on the rock."

Oh Lord, cleaning up the debris is such hard work ... so much rubble, so much destruction. Please help with the clearing away and the rebuilding. Help each one to hear You clearly, to know beyond the shadow of a doubt that You are right there with them and that You care. Guide them and direct them every step of the way. Thank You for Your patient, loving care.

How should you begin?

_____

_____

_____

_____

_____

TANDEM

From the beginning,

A new step,
A one–two, I can–do step.
First a step, then a turn,
A one–two, I can–do step,
Rhythm pulsing,
Fervor building.

A new step,
A one–two, I can–do step.
Watching closely, leaning slightly,
Holding tightly, floating lightly.

A new step,
A one–two, I can–do step.
A promenade, arm around me,
Raboni, Raboni, ever teaching, always tandem.

A new step,
A one–two, we can–do step.

The Bride
Original Oil 30" x 40"

THE BELT OF TRUTH

The thoughts didn't say, "Oh, you could be angry about that." Or, "I bet that makes you afraid." No. They were illusive and scary, bombarding my mind constantly. Zap, zap, zap. They went from worrying about my other children, feeling depressed and overwhelmed, to "if only I had … " and on and on.

I remember walking to work one day, feeling overwhelmed with missing Jason. The only way to make the pain stop was to speak out loud. I started putting on the armor of God from Ephesians 6. "Lord, thank You that I am saved by Your grace. Thank You that Jason is in heaven with You. Thank You that our separation is temporary. Thank You for the breastplate of righteousness. Thank You that I can walk a victorious life. Thank You for the belt of truth. The truth is that heaven is real and that soon enough we will all be together there with You. Thank You for the sword of the Spirit. Thank You that Your Word has answers to all of my problems. Thank You for the shield of faith. Thank You that You will walk with me everyday and that I do not have to handle this alone."

Applying Scriptural truths to my day to day walk became imperative.

- When I was depressed and wanting to melt into the plaid love seat in our bedroom, "The truth is that the same Holy Spirit who raised Jesus from the dead is available to me daily. If He can raise Christ from the dead, He can give me strength for each new day."

- When fighting self pity, "The truth is that I can do all things through Christ, who strengthens me."

- When I'm feeling misunderstood, "The truth is that Jesus understands."

- When I'm feeling all alone, "The truth is that Jesus will never leave me nor forsake me."

- When I'm feeling frightened by the long journey ahead, "The truth is that God has not given me a spirit of fear, but of love and of power and of a sound mind."

- When I'm being anxious about my family, "The truth is that I don't need to be anxious about anything, because by prayer I can let my requests be known to God, and the peace of God which passes all understanding will keep my heart and mind in Christ Jesus."

Knowing the truth was priceless when it came to facing the lies. I found lots of lies lying in the clutter of life after this storm hit. It took time and effort to face each one. Journaling helped. I circled round and round each issue until I could come to grips with it. Being able to go on with my life without being encumbered with the lies was worth the effort.

Some of the major lies were specific to my life, like "Art is a waste of time." But others had a much broader application, like "It would be easier if you divorced." Some lies came in the form of experiences. When we are in the depths of grief, we are an easy target.

Our enemy, the devil, is a crafty imitator. I remember calling out in my ignorance, "Jason, I need you." Now, that seems innocent enough, but the enemy grabbed it as an open door. He sent what I will call a familiar spirit to imitate Jason. I would feel him here, and I welcomed him. It felt good at first. Scripture teaches us to try the spirits. This never crossed my mind in this case until later. The enemy is never going to come in as darkness; he'll imitate light, but the fruit indicates the truth. God sweetly exposed me to teachings on demons, and I immediately questioned the "presence" in my home. It wasn't peaceful here anymore; I got suspicious. It wasn't just me. Our neighbor actually saw him at Christmas time, "skittering" behind the door, like a little imp. Our loved ones DO NOT live here. They DO NOT come back that way. Can they? Does God allow some communication some-times to bless us? Yes, apparently so. Many have experienced this. Hebrews would bear this out also. But it is momentary, a fleeting gift. Not something we should seek after. (Like Wayne's experi-ence in the story, heaven is real.) When we cry out to anyone or anything but the One and only true God, we are asking to be deceived.

God is faithful. He knew my heart. He knew I loved Him. He knew I wanted only to serve Him. He also knew the enemy was deceiving me. Being exposed to the truth about demons and ap-propriating that truth was not an overnight reality. It took much time and study. I share the results with you briefly because I feel it is an important truth and one I have not seen addressed else-where. The Bible tells us very clearly not to seek the dead. Don't. Now, if God chooses to reveal them to us, as He did to Jesus on the mount of transfiguration, HOORAY! But that's his choice. Our heart needs to cling to Jesus. The good news is that if we re-sist the enemy, he must flee. When I came to grips with the spirit issue in my home, I took authority, as God says we can. A friend and I prayed through the entire house. I felt the enemy leave, along with the bickering that had accompanied his presence. Now, because we prayed, our home is full of peace and love. Jesus gives discernment. Jesus lights our path. There is no darkness He cannot overcome. Fear of death, the grave, and the enemy all pale in the light of His truth and His presence.

Jesus heals all the broken places. The truth is that heaven is real, and when I focus on the reality of Christ risen and coming again, there is peace and joy in the midst of sorrow. That is the miracle for now. But later, the miracle will be no more sorrow. My battle cry: "Truth!"

Ephesians 6:14
Stand firm then, with the belt of truth buckled around your waist …

Father, help these dear ones to search out the truth from Your word and to walk in it. Thank you that your word is truth. Amen.

What truths do you need to proclaim?

_____

_____

_____

_____

_____

_____

_____

_____

_____

_____

"A good battle plan:
Knowing the Word of God
and applying it."

Forgiveness flows...

from a heart that understands the price
that was paid for its redemption.

INNER HEALING

For some, the term "inner healing" may be new. Jesus said, "I came to heal the broken-hearted." One of the ways God has done that for me is through the process called inner healing. This is the way that Scripture touches my experiences. When a memory haunts me, or is recurring, I apply the following Scriptural steps.

1. Forgiveness—asking God to forgive me and applying forgiveness to others.
   A. Ask God to forgive me for my part.
   B. Forgive anyone else involved.
   C. Ask God to forgive me for blaming Him (if I have).

2. I know God was there, so I ask Him to show me where He was.

3. I ask Him what lies I've believed.

4. I ask Him to show me what truths He wants me to understand from this memory.

5. I thank Him for setting me free from the lies and for allowing me by the power of His Holy Spirit to walk in the truth.

One such recurring memory to which I applied the inner healing steps occurred when I was probably nine or ten and alone at home in the summer while my mother worked. This memory had nothing to do with Jason's death, nor was it an unhappy memory. It just came to mind often, and I wondered what the significance was. So I asked the Lord. He reminded me of those summer days—I was supposed to clean up the kitchen dishes before Mom returned from work. Of course, I waited until the last minute, and there would usually be wet soap bubbles in the sink when she arrived. Now the memory I had was of the messy kitchen and me feeling guilty. Forgiveness—asking God for it on my own behalf and applying it to others. I asked God to forgive me for my laziness and my procrastination. I asked God to forgive my mom for leaving a sensitive youngster alone so often. I didn't blame God, so I didn't need to ask forgiveness for that.

I know God was there, so I asked Him to show me where He was. The answer came as a picture of me alone in the dining room, with a Monopoly game spread out on the floor. This would have been typical. My friends and I would play this game for hours. I would postpone all my work till the last minute. This always left me a little anxious and guilty.

In the picture, Jesus was in the kitchen, which was piled high with dirty dishes on the counter next to the sink. He was busy dropping all the refuse down the garbage disposal. Then He turned and came and sat down next to me on the floor to play Monopoly.

The lies? God was not angry with me. There was no condemnation for being just on time! I didn't need to feel guilty.

The truth? He wanted to get rid of all my guilt and shame about a lot of things. (We didn't have a garbage disposal in that little house, but God sure wanted to dispose of all my garbage thinking.) Jesus loved me and wanted to spend time with me. Playing is OK!

Lord, thank You for the healing touch. Thank You that it is OK to play. Thank You that there is no condemnation to those who are in Christ Jesus. Thank You for coming that we might have life and enjoy our lives! You will be with me and show me how to balance the work and the play.

Those feelings were huge issues in my life, but they no longer haunt me. Allowing God to touch the hurting spots doesn't remove the memory, but it does relieve the pain. He is incredible!

When it came to Jason's death, there were a number of things that haunted me. The same principles helped.

The day of Jason's accident I was at work. This was a job I had to pray myself into every day. I didn't like the work, but we needed the income. Right about the time of Jason's accident, I've always thought, I was walking downstairs into the break room, grumbling to God about this job. Now, didn't the devil have a field day with this one!

Step 1: Forgiveness
Lord, I'm so sorry for grumbling and complaining about that job. You know how I struggled daily to give You thanks for the income and all it supplied for our family and yet how much I hated the position.

Forgive anyone involved:
I choose to forgive myself for grumbling and complaining and for anything that may have been set forth in the spiritual realm as a result.

Step 2: Where were you, Lord?
After much prayer on this one, I still couldn't see Him; I finally realized He was right behind me with His hands on my shoulders.

Step 3: What lies have I been believing?
Lies: It was your fault.
Somehow I caused the accident.
I was being punished.

Step 4: What is the truth Jesus wants me to know?
Truth: Jesus was in control; I don't have that kind of power! I was in Neenah! I wasn't there!
Jesus was with me.
Jesus was walking me out of that job.

Thank You Lord. You do not deal with us according to our sins. Thank You for setting me free once again from lies and condemnation. Thank You for providing for us through work I love. You are wonderful and faithful, loving and kind. Your peace is the best gift. Amen.

Psalm 29:11

The LORD gives strength to his people;
the LORD blesses his people with peace.

Dear Father, help me face the pain so You can heal me. Amen.

Are there memories you need to deal with?

_____

_____

_____

_____

_____

_____

_____

_____

_____

_____

_____

Walking in the Sunshine

A TIME
TO DANCE

HEAVEN NOTES

The Bible is full of references to heaven, and there are many good books about the subject. So this is just to encourage you to spend more time thinking about the wonders to come. There will be no more crying, no more disease, no more tears. There will be a wonderful banquet with our loving heavenly father. There will be peace and joy and holiness. There will be incredible beings and angels beyond counting. There will be kingdoms to reign over. There will be words of praise for works done on Earth. There will be a river of life, a New Jerusalem. There will be rejoicing with the angels. There will be a home for all of us who call on the name of Jesus. There will be the presence of God himself and Jesus on the throne. We cannot even imagine the glory, majesty, beauty or joy. It will be our forever home, along with those we love so dearly.

Colossians 3:2–4
Set your minds on things above, not on earthly things. For you died, and your life is now hidden with Christ in God. When Christ, who is your life, appears, then you also will appear with him in glory.

Revelations 21:3–4
And I heard a loud voice from the throne saying, "Now the dwelling of God is with men, and he will live with them. They will be his people, and God himself will be with them and be their God. He will wipe every tear from their eyes. There will be no more death or mourning or crying or pain, for the old order of things has passed away.

Father, thank You for the hope of heaven. Help me keep my thoughts on things above. Amen.

Have you thought about how wonderful heaven is going to be?

_____

_____

_____

_____

_____

_____

_____

_____

_____

"Heaven is connected to here—
eternity doesn't start
at the end of time."

MARTI

I just got off the phone with Marti. It's been almost 18 years since Jason died, and she has been my friend for all of that time. Marti has prayed faithfully for our family since before we met. My lashes are still damp from the tears I shed as we prayed together today. Her kidney has failed—Jason's kidney.

When we were asked whether we would be willing for Jason to be an organ donor, our reply was "Yes, yes of course." It just seemed the right thing to do. Someone would be helped. We weren't thinking past our pain to the results of this action.

When I received a letter of thanks from Marti, I was amazed. I didn't expect one. It was so kind of her to take the trouble to communicate with us. The university hospital had strict privacy codes, so she had to contact us through them. She didn't know our name, or Jason's. "I am a married mother of 33 with two children, ages six and seven, a boy and a girl, respectively. I greatly appreciate the added years I have received through the kidney/pancreas transplant, as does my family and my husband's family. May God protect and guide you and your family as you grieve, and know that you will always be in my prayers. God will know where those prayers belong."

As time went on we gave each other our addresses and phone numbers. When we had occasion to be near their home, they invited us to join them for dinner and time to connect. I am still in awe of the blessing. Here before us was a woman, a veritable stranger and yet so connected at the heart. She was healthy and happy, and so appreciative. It was a gift to be with them, to see one more thing God was working for good.

While we were talking, Marti mentioned how her hair had changed. It had become curly. As we said our goodbyes, and I hugged her close, I felt her hair at the nape of her neck ... it was just like Jason's, curly and a little coarse. Tears I couldn't identify, not sorrow, not joy ... thankful for the good, thankful for the connection.

I hadn't heard from her in some time, and she kept coming to mind, so I called her. She was apologetic: "How do you tell someone a thing like this?" She reassured me that for a transplant to last 17 years was very good. She is so thankful for the healthy years she's had. So am I. She has prayed for us all these years. Now it's my turn to pray for Marti.

Philippians 1:3
I thank my God every time I remember you.

Dear Lord, thank You for the blessing Marti has been to our family. Thank You that through our sorrow Marti has had time to raise her children. Lord, help us to see the good in our difficult circumstances. May You be glorified in all things. Amen.

Is there someone in need of your prayer?

_____

_____

_____

_____

_____

_____

_____

_____

_____

TRUTH RIVER

The eternal God of the universe loves you individually
and completely.
He wants to comfort and caress away the tears.
He wants to walk with you every day.
He wants to share His life-giving Spirit with you.
He wants to laugh and cry with you in an intimate, personal way.
He wants to bless you with life abundantly.
He wants to free you from the lies of your past.
He wants to fill you with hope for today and all your tomorrows.
He wants to fill you with joy unspeakable and full of glory.
He wants to fill your heart with love and beauty.
He wants you to be filled with the fullness of God.
He wants to direct your paths and light your way.
He wants to remove all fear and doubt.
He wants to scrub you clean.
He wants to welcome you home.
God will make good come from this.
Heaven is better than here.
In heaven, we will all be together—forever.
This is a temporary separation.
The Holy Spirit will give you the same resurrection power that
raised Jesus from the dead to live your life now.
Our God is a mighty God.
Sin, death and Satan are my enemies—no one else.
God loves you, God loves you, God loves you.

2 Timothy 3:16
All Scripture is God-breathed and is useful for teaching, rebuk-
ing, correcting and training in righteousness.

Lord, please help us to live in the truth of Your love. Amen.

New Normal
Original Oil 16" x 12"

Do you need to soak in the Truth River?

_____

_____

_____

_____

_____

_____

_____

_____

Thank you, Lord!
I feel overwhelmed by your love.

VIEW FROM THE HILL

The sun will never shine again
The sun is shining still, and when you heal, it won't make you angry that the world still goes on.

I know the plans I have for you. (Jeremiah 29:11)

I'll never be happy again
Happy is a state of mind. Roger Miller used to sing "You can't roller skate in a buffalo herd, but you can be happy if you've a mind to." When you have healed you will be able to choose to be happy again.

This is the day the LORD has made, I will rejoice and be glad in it. (Psalm 118:24)

I'll never be able to overcome this
Overcoming anything on our own can be a daunting task.

God's Word says that I can do all things through Christ who strengthens me. I may not feel like I can, but God is true to His Word.

I'll never be able to function again
Not only can you exist, but you can live a full and happy life.

I can do all things through Christ who strengthens me. (Philippians 4:13 NKJV)

I can't do this
What we really mean is that we can't continue to hurt like this. We can't deal with the thought of this kind of pain going on and on and on. It won't. Take one step at a time.

Each day has enough trouble of its own. (Matthew 6:34)

Nobody understands

Jesus does. It is no small thing that the God of all creation, the God of the universe, who holds everything in His hands, loves you, totally understands you, and promises to be with you.

I will never leave you or forsake you. (Joshua 1:5)

I have to do this all alone

When Jesus left this earth, he said, "I will send you the comforter." The Holy Spirit will be your guide, your friend, and your support. (see John 14:16–18)

Blessed are those who mourn for they shall be comforted. I've discovered the comfort is God Himself … a deeper peace, a deeper love, a deeper joy, because of His love filling the void.

Some steps are bigger – some more confident …

But the important thing is to keep walking.

Dear Body of Christ,

On behalf of all the grieving souls out there, please be encouraged that you can make a difference. Please pray, listen to the Holy Spirit and be obedient. If a hurting person is on your mind day and night, besides praying, ask the Lord what He would have you do, and then do it...a phone call, a hug, a meal, an errand, or maybe babysitting. It may be very small in your eyes, but even the simplest daily tasks can be overwhelming to someone in deep sorrow. Please also understand that though the first year is very difficult, grieving for a child or a mate doesn't magically end in a year. Three to five years is a much more realistic estimate of how long it takes to pick up your life again. The grieving (defined as deep sorrow) is definitely not confined to a tidy 365-day year. Because that is true, you can show much compassion by being thoughtful and considerate of another's pain much beyond that first year.

From an evangelistic perspective, Christians are missing a huge opportunity to show the love of Christ to a hurting world. Not only are there massive needs during the grieving process, but during this time our own mortality, especially if we don't know Christ, looms before us. Now, if Christians assume the world's viewpoint and are afraid of not only death but of the pain it causes in others, we render ourselves useless in this vast arena. What other event is there that everyone on this Earth will face? I hope you will examine your own views on death and dying, overcome your fears, and move forward in the love of Christ to bring hope and healing to those around you.

May God richly bless you for your compassion.

In His love,

Peg Muenzel

TRAIL NOTES ~ JOURNAL ENTRIES

The two-plus years have been full of growth. I've never worked so hard in my life. Thank You, Jesus, for being here, being near. Thank You for the knowledge that I can walk in victory because of You. Thank You for the holiness You call us to and the life giving Holy Spirit to accomplish it. Thank You, Holy Spirit, for Your abiding, loving presence in my life.

30 months

Lord, thank you that the pain isn't so intense that it overshadows everything else anymore.

32 months

Oh, I need to paint. I just want to swish it around, watch the colors move ...

35 months

Shame is paralyzing, making me completely immobile. It's like not being able to catch your breath with your mind. Shame is not from God, so I do not need to accept it.

Insight—Romans 1:20

For since the creation of the world his invisible attributes, his eternal power and divine nature, have been clearly seen, being understood through what has been made, so that they are without excuse.

Eternal power—the wind, the oceans, the earth turning—divine nature—His beauty, orderliness, creativity, diversity, majesty, gentleness, humor, wisdom, intelligence—loving and peaceful, sometimes angry. We can know about God's attributes by observing His creation. The art reflects the artist.

3rd year anniversary time

It's June, and the 26th is approaching with lots of memories pushing, forcing themselves on me. I don't want to think about the accident, the loss. I love Jason, but the memories make me sad and I play them back and I think, oh, I should have done this or that differently and I don't like it. That day can't hurt me. No, and neither can anything else without passing through my Father's hands. Oh Lord, give me wisdom and guidance, please, on how to best handle these days. I need a Psalm. Psalm 11—In the Lord I take refuge ... for the Lord is righteous. He loves the righteous. The upright will behold His face. I love You, Lord. Please fill me today with Your Spirit. May I overflow with Your love today.

Lord, You're the One who understands, who'll pray for me, hug me, wipe my tears, and fill me again with strength and joy. So that's the plan for now. I'm exhausted—I need to be here with You—on my little love seat—quietly waiting for You to soothe my troubled heart, wash away the pain, and put on the healing balm of Your Spirit, like the fresh, cool breeze blowing through this window—refreshing, cool, peaceful and comforting. I love You, Lord. Help, please. Amen.

June 27th

The Lord understands my very first plaintive cry for more good to come from this terrible loss—good meaning, eternal good. Kingdom growth! When Jesus came to suffer and die, there was a purpose—a huge purpose. God did not take the death of His Son lightly and neither do I. My prayer is for good—much eternal good to come from this. I know that God, my loving heavenly Father, will say yes to that prayer in more ways than I'll ever see.

What He's done for others, He'll do for you

June 30th (from hymn book)

Oh, Lord, how this song speaks to my heart!

O Love That Wilt Not Let Me Go
George Matheson
Albert L. Peace

Oh, Love that wilt not let me go,
I rest my weary soul in thee;
I give thee back the life I owe, that
In thine ocean depths its flow may richer, fuller be.

O Light that followest all my way,
I yield my flickering torch to Thee;
My heart restores its borrowed ray,
That in thy sunshine's blaze its day
May brighter, fairer be.

O Joy that seekest me thru pain,
I cannot close my heart to Thee;
I trace the rainbow thru' the rain,
And feel the promise is not vain
That morn shall tearless be.

O Cross that liftest up my head,
I dare not ask to hide from Thee;
I lay in dust life's glory dead,
And from the ground there blossoms red
Life that shall endless be.

Beyond Year Three

July 1, (about light)

The brighter the light—the deeper the shadows—they become more defined—when the light is obscure, so are the shadows—when the light is direct, the shadows are obvious and defined. Pray for the direct light—In the presence of God there is no darkness. There are areas that have been obscure, that need to come to the light—as the light approaches shadows are long, when directly overhead, short—less area covered—less darkness—Pray for direct light. Direct light is illuminating, warming, comforting, pure, enlightening, invigorating, exciting, bright, pure, stimulating.

July

Thank You for the breeze and peace and comfort and joy. Thank You that it's better, so much better now. Though the pain can be intense, deep and sorrowful—it isn't constant, and I know that though its depth scares me sometimes—I know You'll see me through. And I think that the pain is deeper inside now, more internalized—different. And I wonder sometimes whether it's the magnitude of the hurt or the lack of pain surrounding it right now, or both. Like a black shape on white paper is so much starker than if there were more black on the paper. So healing is good even if the stark reality catches you off guard sometimes—or rather the depth of the hurt from the stark reality KNOCKS you off guard.

John 16:33

These things I have spoken to you, that in me you may have peace. In the world you have tribulation, but take courage; I have overcome the world.

Pain is more startling when it
isn't constant.

December

I feel as though I have reached a plateau in my grief. Maybe it
will get better from here—hard to say since I haven't been here
before. But I feel like I am functioning again. It's an effort, but
I can. The pain that I have now is contained. I mean it doesn't
flood all over me all the time. Sometimes it is overwhelming,
but not as often. Mostly, it's a gentle presence—a sensitive area
inside that feels the pain almost separated from my conscious-
ness. So sometimes I am aware, and sometimes I am not. I can
purposely visit if I wish. Sometimes I am pitched into it but not
as often, and I am not afraid of it. I know it is temporary. I can
identify the pain, sadness, loneliness and sorrow now. They are

separate entities not all mashed together in a bloody mass. It was ugly, now, more precious. A part of my Jason memories. To be touched by the hand of God is an incredible thing. He brings healing, love and joy, comfort, peace ... a stirring of life again within my soul. Precious in the sight of the Lord is the death of his saints. Amen.

There are longer periods between the grief episodes now, which is a relief, but then when I'm having a bad time it sometimes takes me longer to spot what's going on. Before I always knew it was grief—it was so constant. Sometimes I need to cry or rest or whatever instead of just pushing on with life activities.

The healing is in God's hands ... so smile—Lighten up!

More in December

My grieving is different again—very deep—an intense missing when I acknowledge it. It's more prevalent again now. Is it the holidays or because it's been a while. I do not think every hour— Jason's gone—or maybe even every day. The grieving times seem to come in "bunches," and this is a rather large one.

January

I'm thinking now very much of the future—of life. When I think of Jason, I think of how much I love him more than how much I miss him, and I think of the future and eternity with him more than the present without him, more of my life and what the Lord is doing than of Jason and our loss. Jason, from the time he was a baby, lived his life with gusto—and now I see me being free to do the same.

I felt like wet linen Sunday—just needing to be aired—have the wind blow life back into my limp, wet form.

Year Four

It's not the living of the life that makes it valuable, but the essence of the life—the creation. The creation itself is valuable, more valuable than anything else and very, very loved by the Creator.

Spring—about writing this book

Am having such an emotional struggle, I thought I would make note of it. The going back in my memory to tell of the events surrounding Jason's death felt like I was taking a subway trip down, down deep into the recesses of my pain and I couldn't get out— that upon arriving I'd given up my ticket to get back to here, to the safety of distance that I've achieved through time. The memories all want to come along back with me. I don't want them to. I have to "go back" in order to write. It's so exhausting I can't stay long, and the journey back is all uphill. I can't just flip a switch and be in the present. It would be good if I could go back in the subway, stay in the car, and just observe through the window and not be hurt all over again by the pain I'm traveling through.

Somewhere between years five and seven I was having tea with a dear friend. Suddenly, she had one of those indescribable, insightful moments and said, "Peggy, you're back."

"Yes." I replied, and I knew it was true. In every way I was back, stronger and different, but whole, happy and healed. Back from the valley of the shadow of death. YEAH!!!

Springtime Comes ⋯

P.S.

Dear Ones,

It's been 18 years now since our Jason left us. I want to add one final note of encouragement to you. Wayne and I are happy. My life is full. We have two darling granddaughters and a grandson. Our children live near by and are a constant source of joy. In the summer we are blessed to relax at our cabin in the north woods of Wisconsin. Best of all, I'm painting again! I have a studio in our home. I crank up whatever music I'm in the mood for, from Christian worship music, 60s rock 'n' roll or classical, and anything in between. Or, I take my things and head outdoors. God's beautiful world inspires me. Creating art blesses me.

The painting (shown between pages 130 and 131) that I call "New Normal" reflects my life right now. I'm in flux. I've retired from teaching art at a Christian school. I have enjoyed speaking for various women's groups and love mission trips, but I really don't know where God is taking me next. It's OK. I'm content. Our "new normal" is very different from what I envisioned our life would be.

I didn't think I could ever be happy again ... I was wrong. But I was right about the process. Crying was good. Grieving was necessary. God was faithful. He did have a plan for me, to give me a future and a hope. He has no favorites. He will be faithful to you too.

God bless you on your journey. I'm praying peace and joy for you.

Love in Him,

Peg Muenzel

GRIEF RESOURCES

- Alan D. Wolfelt, Ph.D. C.T. Internationally noted author, educator and grief coun-selor. Founder: Center for Loss and Life Transition, Fort Collins, Colorado. Dr. Wolfelt offers trainings, books and resources. http://www.centerforloss.com

- *A Grief Observed* (HarperOne) by C.S. Lewis

- *Mourning Song* (Fleming H. Revell) by Joyce Landorf Heatherley

- *The Dance of Life: Weaving Sorrows and Blessings into One Joyful Step* (Ava Maria Press) by Henri Nouwen

- *Our Greatest Gift: A Meditation on Dying and Caring* (HarperOne) by Henri Nouwen

- *In the Presence of Grief* (The Guilford Press) by Dorothy Bevcar

- *God in the Dark* (Regent College Publishing) by Luci Shaw

- *Harsh Grief Gentle Hope* (Navpress Publishing Group) by Mary White

- *Help Me to Remember* by Dennis Jernigan http://www.dennisjernigan.com

- *Streams in the Desert* (Zondervan) by Mrs. Charles Cowman

- *Living When a Loved One Has Died* (Beacon Press) by Earl Grollman

- *Parental Loss of a Child* (Research Press) by Therese Rando

- *Recovering from the Losses of Life* (Revell) by H. Norman Wright

- *The Grief Recovery Handbook* (Harper) by John James and Russell Friedman

- *The Reluctant Traveler: A Pilgrimage Through Loss and Recovery* (Navpress) by Diane Dempsey Marr, Ph.D

- *Talking About Death* (Beacon Press) by Grollman/Avishai

- *Unspoken Grief: Coping with Childhood Sibling Loss* (Lexington Books) by Helen Rosen

This list of resources has been graciously supplied by Practical Family Living Website (www.pfl.org). Radio programs, resources and articles by the therapists at The Center for Family Healing, Menasha, Wisconsin.

ABOUT THE AUTHOR

Life is a celebration of the creative process for Peg Muenzel. Her paintings showcase her enjoyment of beauty with a connection to concepts reaching deep into the human soul. Peg's commissioned murals as well as paintings are treasured locally as well as internationally. She prays that this, her first book, will be used as an instrument of healing for those who are hurting.

Peg took her first oil painting class after her son Jason was born. It was love at first swish of color on the canvas. Finding the time to create began as a struggle filling many journal pages as she grappled with art and its place in her life. Finally one day she begged God to give her insight. His response was, "You are looking at art as if it is a wedding cake." In her heart she knew what He meant. For her, art was wonderful, but in the scheme of life, not necessary—a contradiction to the creative, artistic God we serve!

Her journey of discovery began many years ago, when God took a young lady who loved Him—but had many insecurities and fears—and fashioned her into a delightful, encouraging, loving woman. Peg's experience leading a local women's ministry and serving on its national board—as well as training through other groups—taught her the value of prayer and teamwork. It also honed her skills in public speaking and prayer ministry.

Peg married Wayne (her high school sweetheart!) 40-some years ago when he was in the army, stationed in England. When asked about her husband she says, "I've watched this dear, gentle man walk through pain and hardship with a dignity that kings might envy. He encourages me when I struggle, prays for me when I'm weak, holds me when I cry and cheers me when in doubt." Wayne is her constant friend and companion whose humor brightens the lives of many. The couple resides in Neenah, Wisconsin.

Peg cherishes being a mother. As a stay at home mom it often felt like swimming upstream, but her experiences growing up as a "latch key kid" (before there was such a term) helped form her decision. She loved every part of being a mom—creating home made gifts, making costumes and clothes as well as decorating. But most of all she appreciated being there for her precious brood. Today her three grown children and grandchildren live nearby and fill her life with laughter and tremendous joy. Spending time with them, especially at their lake cabin, replenishes her. She considers her family her most priceless gift saying: "Raising them was the one time in my life when I knew I was doing the most important job in the world." Their love and encouragement in the book writing process has been precious to her.

In 1992, Peg's life was shattered by the tragic and unexpected death of her son Jason. In the pages of this book you will find a love letter between her Lord, herself and her son. Through faith in Jesus she chronicles her journey through grief. With candor and an artistic voice, Peg details how God's Word and Spirit brought her to a place of hope and healing.

This is more than a grief book, it is a tool of healing—a deep look into a mother's broken heart, and a plat map of sorts that helps lead others from the unthinkable to the unexpected.

Peg works as an artist, author and speaker—combining art, music and drama. She is also an engaging speaker for women's groups, retreats and other functions. She draws audiences into personal places of reflection and healing using her artwork to illustrate her message and express her heart.

Visit www.PegMuenzel.com.